- The LARGEST C(food and food-anywhere.

- EASY TO USE. M~~~~~~~~~~~ words where you expect them.

- Hundreds of Spanish words & phrases used in cooking instructions and on packet food.

- Special section for those on Special Diets for ALLERGIES and INTOLERANCES. With Personal Safety Sheet.

- Lots of U.S English terms. For ALL English speakers.

- A MUST for English-speaking restaurateurs and shop owners.

- Perfecto para cocineros de la COCINA INTERNACIONAL que ofrecen MENUS.

- KNOW what you are eating - never eat a criadilla by mistake!

For Mal, Viv, Tasha, and Kitty.

Thanks to my wife, Mal, for suffering much of the endless proof-reading and checking with me. She hates that sort of thing.

Thanks also, for their help and friendship to:

> Mark Worsley
> James Ure
> Julie Sothern
> Andrew Pilkington
> Reggie Lau
> Alan Hess
> Trevor Chadwick
> Bill Calloway
> Linda Brindle
> Pat Bresnen
> Alex Biezaneck

(Having spent all my school years near the end of every choosing due to the tyranny of the alphabet, the above list in reverse alphabetical order.)

The English/Spanish A to Z of FOOD Cookery and Shopping

Written, compiled, and designed by

Paul Ure

Published by Whitestreak © 2005
Copyright © Paul Ure 2005

The right of Paul Ure to be identified as the author of this work has been asserted by him in accordance with the Copyright, Designs, and Patents Act, 1988

No part of this book may be copied or reproduced by any means or stored on a retrieval system or transmitted in any form or by whatever means without the prior permission of the publisher.

August 2005

Depósito Legal: MA-297-2006
ISBN: 0-9551213-0-2

Whitestreak, Whitestreak Publishing, and the Whitestreak logo are copyright © Paul Ure 2005.
All graphics are the property of the author.

Whereas everything has been done to achieve accuracy, no responsibility can be accepted by the author or publishers for any problems arising out of any information contained herein.

CONTENTS

Introduction 6

Key to Layout 9

Basic Pronunciation 11

ENGLISH / SPANISH 17

SPANISH / ENGLISH 70

Wine 146
    Sweetness Scale 147

Shopping 148
    English / Spanish 149
    Spanish / English 155

Numbers 158

SPECIAL DIETS 160
    Allergies & Intolerances 161
    Problem Foods & Additives 163

Spanish Meat Cuts
    Beef 166
    Pork 167
    Lamb 168

From the author 169

Personal safety sheet 170

Introduction

Some translations for food and dishes are commonly applied, but many are not exact matches. For example, *ternera* is always translated as veal, but it is not the same as British veal. Spanish calves grow almost to maturity, so ternera is more like British beef. That which the British would call veal - from a young animal, is either ternera *joven* (young), ternera *menor* (junior), ternera *lechal* (suckling), ternera *blanca* (white), or ternera *de Avila*. The paler the meat, the younger the animal.

Spain is a big country with distinct regions and customs. Consequently, many items have more than one name, and there are more words for stew than you can shake a wooden spoon at. Also, one species of fish may have multiple names, and different species can share the same name, and the various names for shrimps, prawns, crayfish, and lobsters sometimes seem wholly interchangeable.

Bacon has several names, one of which is *panceta*. However, the word panceta itself includes several items, one of which is what the British know as belly pork, which is raw and uncured.

Turrón is always translated as nougat, but of the many, many kinds that exist, you won't find the chewy white or pink stuff you may remember from childhood. You will, though, find some that resemble the nutty, bitty nougat that came in boxes of chocolates. Ignore the claim that it is all based on ground almonds because you will find many variants that clearly aren't; chocolate with crispy rice (*arroz inflado*), for instance, regularly appears.

Bocadillo is commonly translated as sandwich, but it is not the large-white-sliced, triangular sandwich of Britain. These do exist, but they are mainly for foreigners. This isn't surprising as freshly-baked Spanish bread is arguably the best in Europe. It is also always available as many *panaderías* (bakeries) remain open through siesta, and many petrol stations have in-store ovens. A bocadillo is a filled roll. Small rolls are called *bocaditos*. Other terms include, *sandwich*, *sanwich*, and *emparedado*.

Empanadas (pies) have little in common with the British variants. Flat slabs of pastry with a sandwich-like spread of tuna and tomato, or *pisto* (mixed cooked vegetables), inside. ***Empanadillas*** (small pies) are bite-sized deep-fried parcels filled with such as spinach or tuna, the pastry of which is more like that of samosas. The shortcrust, deep-filled pies of the UK are, in Spain, mostly frozen imports, or are produced by ex-pat bakers.

There is no difference in name between chips and crisps - both are ***patatas fritas***.

While there may be a lot of egg in a ***tortilla***, it is not the main ingredient, as in the British omelette. It is there primarily to hold the potato (*patata*) and all the other ingredients together. The mainly-egg omelette is attributed to France - *tortilla francesa*.

A common title included in many different dishes and packaged foods is "Quatro Estaciones". This is derived from *estaciones del año - seasons of the year*, and simply means a wide variety of ingredients. Such dishes may include all the different meats - fish, seafood, bird, and mammal, and several types of vegetable. It can also be applied to a mixture of salad leaves, or vegetables without meat.

Some items have no UK equivalent, and translations, though perhaps not exact, will point you in the right direction to discover, for instance, that it's not a fish but a bread product.

Many Spanish words have several, unrelated meanings. For example, *manzana* means apple, knob, and a block of buildings. Unless the others are useful or interesting, only the food-related translations are given.

Translations given indicate the meaning or common usage - which may not be the literal translation. For example, *Lo siento* means, *I am sorry*. Its literal translation, though, is, *It I feel - I feel it*.

The two main sections of the book do not contain exactly the same number of translations. The Spanish/English section lists every discovered translation for a particular item, whereas the English/Spanish section lists only the minimum number of translations necessary to distinguish any item nationally. Also, the Spanish/English section contains many words that the English speaker would never look for in the English/Spanish section, such as the very many types of fish and seafood that will never be seen in a British fishmonger's, and the unique wine terminology.

Cooking

The Spanish/English section also contains common words and terms used in cooking instructions. Recipes from many sources - recipe books, cookery magazines, and packet foods, have been used to provide the included words and phrases.

When using the book to translate cooking instructions, bear in mind that different writers use different styles of instruction. One may say, "*now* do this", another, "*then* do this". Similarly, one may write, "*we* then do this", another, "*you* then do this". These slight differences change the words used, though the root term remains the same. Mostly, it is the ending that alters, so look for similarities in the beginning of new words. If you come across a word that begins like one listed, it will likely be a change of tense, part of speech, etc – usually.

Key To Layout

It is hoped that the presentation within is both obvious and intuitive, but the following examples explain the details. Please note that the examples may not exactly match the entries in the main body – they are examples for instruction only.

bacon .... *bacon*; *beicon*; *panceta*.

Three different translations for bacon.

paprika .... *pimentón*;
                               pimiento colorado.

Two different names for paprika, but limited line space forces the list onto the next line. The semi-colon separates the distinct entries, and indicates more to come. The full stop indicates end of entry. So *pimentón* and *pimiento colorado* both mean *paprika*.

egg .... *huevo*.
   beaten .... *huevo batido*.
   hard-boiled .... *huevo duro\cocido*.

Words separated by "\" are shared by the other words in the entry. Here it indicates separate endings for *huevo*, so *huevo duro* and *huevo cocido* both mean hard-boiled egg.

The indented *beaten* and *hard-boiled*, relate to the *egg* above – so *beaten egg* is *huevo batido*, and *hard-boiled egg* is *huevo duro* or\and *huevo cocido*.

Indented words always link to the next *level* above, not to the *words* above if they are similarly indented.

Indented words can either precede or follow the root word, but if there is any possible confusion where they precede the root, the indented entry includes the root-word, or some portion of it if space is limited, to indicate sequence.

> *bottle* .... *botella.*
>   *feeding bottle* ..... *tetera; biberon de bebe.*
>   *opener* .... *decapsulador.*

If the root word, *bottle*, had not been added after *feeding*, the meaning could have been misconstrued – *bottle feeding*. If there is no likely confusion, the root word is not added.

> *clove* .... *clavo (de comer).*

Brackets give additional information. Spanish often applies its descriptive words to other items which bear similar characteristics. The main meaning of ***clavo*** is nail. Labels on packs or jars of cloves rarely give the ***de comer***, but elsewhere it may be needed for clarity. A clove of garlic is ***diente de ajo***, so that will not be a source of confusion. (*Diente*, incidentally, means *tooth*, and *diente de leon* is dandelion.)

Order throughout is strictly alphabetical by the left columns, regardless of punctuation, spaces, etc.

> <u>*ala*</u> .... *wing.*
> <u>*a la b*</u>*rasa* .... *charcoal grilled.*
> <u>*alacha*</u> .... *large sardine.*
> <u>*a la p*</u>*arrilla* .... *grilled.*

Basic Pronunciation

Although we share an alphabet (mostly), the sounds, individually and in combination, frequently differ. Getting the pronunciation right is more than half the battle in being understood. Even with the correct words, you will not be understood if you get the pronunciation seriously wrong.

The Very, Very Quick Guide.

If you don't go on to read the next section; *The Accurate But Still Quite Quick Guide*, at least read this page.

In English all vowel sounds are either short or long.

Short	Long
c<u>a</u>t	l<u>a</u>te
p<u>e</u>t	sc<u>e</u>ne
s<u>i</u>t	k<u>i</u>te
h<u>o</u>t	n<u>o</u>te
p<u>u</u>t	m<u>u</u>te

When speaking in Spanish, forget the Long. (The sounds do exist, but they are not produced using the same letters or methods.)

Pronounce **i** as "*ee*", **u** as "*oo*", **c** before **i** and **e** as "*th*" in **th**in, elsewhere as in **c**ard, **z** also as "*th*" in **th**in, imagine clearing your throat for **x**, **j**, and **g**, and say double **l** as "*y*" in **y**ear. And ...

For pairs of vowels, pronounce each individually, so that the English word *pail* would be *pah-eel*, and *date* would be *dah-teh*. It helps to view English words in this way for fun and experience. It also helps to adopt a Spanish accent - you may feel uneasy, but it really can help understanding.

This isn't perfect, but it will get you a lot closer to the Spanish way.

The Accurate But Still Quite Short Guide.

To give some idea of just how important pronunciation is, imagine you've met a Spanish gentleman who knew the English words, but could only pronounce them in the Spanish way. You might hear,

"Eeahbeh bahkacheh bekowseh ee fehyeh eena oogeh oleh."

See page 14 to understand what he meant.

a - always short as in c<u>a</u>t. Never as in t<u>a</u>me. (*ah in practice examples.*)

e - always short as in p<u>e</u>t. Never as in sc<u>e</u>ne. Not exactly "*ay*" at the end of a word, rather somewhere between p<u>e</u>t and "*ay*". (*eh in examples.*)

i - "*ee*" as sl<u>ee</u>p, but as in p<u>i</u>n is ok. Never as in f<u>i</u>ne.

o - as in h<u>o</u>t. (*oh in examples.*)

u - "*oo*" as in h<u>oo</u>p. [euro = *eh-oo-roh*]. Silent following q and g.
ü means that it is always "*oo*", and is not affected by any pairings or other rules. Never as in <u>u</u>se or p<u>u</u>re.

y - varies; either as in <u>y</u>ear, or as "*ee*", like English happ<u>y</u>. You may also hear it as a soft "j" (as in just) particularly at the beginning of a word. Y on its own means "and", and is simply "*ee*".

b - like English as in <u>b</u>ut.

c - varies: before **e** and **i** as "*th*" in <u>th</u>in, otherwise as in <u>c</u>ard.

ch - like English as in <u>ch</u>ill. [leche (milk) = *leh-cheh*]. (Given its own section in Spanish dictionaries, following C.)

d - as English, but when at the end of a word more like "*dth*", with the tongue touching the back of the upper teeth.

g - similar to English as in <u>g</u>ood, but more strongly aspirated following **e** and **i**. A bit like clearing your throat. (*kh in examples*).
[galleta (biscuit) = g*a-yeh-tah*, congelado (frozen) = *con-khe-lah-doh*].

h - silent. [hielo (ice) = *ee-el-oh*].

ll - "*y*" as in <u>y</u>ear. [calle (street) is *kah-yeh*]. You may also hear it as a soft "*j*" (as in <u>j</u>ust) when at the beginning of a word. (Given its own section in Spanish dictionaries, following L.)

ñ - as "*ny*". [mañana (tomorrow) = *mah-nyah-nah*]. (Given its own section in Spanish dictionaries, following N.)
qu - as English **k**. [quiero (I want) = *kee-eh-roh*.]
r - as English but with a slight roll.
rr - as English, but strongly rolled. Note *pero* (but), and *perro* (dog): the roll distinguishes them. If you can't produce the roll, linger longer on the "*r*" sound.
v - somewhere between English **b** and **v**, with slight emphasis on the **b**.
z - "*th*" as in "**th**in" not as in "**th**an". [zapato (shoe) = *tha-pat-oh*].
j, x - These are special cases as there are no English equivalents, although the throat-clearing sound is common to many other languages. The Scottish ending, "*ch*", as in lo**ch** is close, but with more emphasis on the "*h*" sound. The **j** is never as in **j**ust. ("*kh*" *in examples.*)

Vowel-pairs have distinct sounds based on relative "strengths". A, E, and O are strong, while U and I are weak. Each strong vowel is distinctly sounded:

    ae paella (rice dish) = *pah-eh-yah*,
    ao bacalao (cod) = *bah-kah-lah-oh*
    ea hornear (to bake) = *or-neh-ar*
    eo fideos (fine noodles) = *fid-eh-oss*

Combinations of strong and weak vowels, and of weak-only vowels, produce individual sounds:

    ai as eye - faisán (pheasant) = *fy-san*
    au *ow* in c*ow* - laurel (bayleaf) = *low-rel*
    ei *ay* as h*ay* – seis (six) = *sayss*
    ou as *oo* – canteloupo (melon) = *can-teh-loo-poh*
    ui *wee* – anguila (eel) = *an-gwee-lah*
         Note that u following q belongs to the q, so:
         mantequilla (butter) = *man-teh-kee-yah*,
         not *man-teh-kwee-yah.*
    iu *yoo* – ciudad (city) = *thew-dad*

Accented letters, á, é, í, ó, ú, indicate where in the word you should place the emphasis. Where there is no accented character, place the emphasis on the second-to-last syllable when the word ends in a vowel (a,e,i,o,u,y), and on the last syllable for words ending with a consonant.

mañana (tomorrow *or* morning) = mah-**nyah**-nah
bocadillo (sandwich) = boh-kah-**dee**-yoh
Málaga = **Mah**-lah-gah
champiñon (mushroom) = sham-pee-**nyon**
yogur (yoghurt) = (ee)-yoh-**goor**

Bueno (good) is *b<u>oo</u>-en-oh*, rather than just *bwen-oh*. The "*oo*" sound should be there, but briefly. Likewise, the "*ee*" part of **y** wants to be felt. *Yema* (egg yolk) should be *ee-yem-ah*, rather than simply *yem-ah*. Just a hint will do. (oo) and (ee) in examples.

One problem with getting the pronunciation right is the complicated reply that comes back at you at a hundred miles an hour. Memorise the phrase, "***Despacio, por favor.***" - it means "***Slowly, please.***"

So, what was the Spanish chap saying?

Eeabeh	I have
bakacheh	backache
bekowseh	because
ee	I
fehyeh	fell
eena	in a
oogeh	huge
oleh	hole

You wouldn't have understood him. The reverse will apply if you pronounce Spanish words in the English way.

Practice Examples

ahumado (smoked) = ah-oo-**mah**-doh
alli (there) = **ah**-yee
anticuado (out of date) = an-tee-**kwah**-doh
berenjena (aubergine) = beh-ren-**khen**-ah
caballa (mackerel) kah-**bah**-yah
cuánto (how much) = k(oo)-**ahn**-toh
cuchara (spoon) = koo-**chah**-rah
cuchillo (knife) = koo-**chee**-yoh
dátil (date [fruit]) = **dah**-teel
doce (twelve) = **doh**-theh
hierbabuena (mint) ee-err-bah-b(oo)-**en**-ah
mantequilla (butter) = man-teh-**kee**-yah
merluza (hake) = mehr-**loo**-thah
molinillo (mill) = moh-lee-**nee**-yoh
naranja (orange) = nah-**ran**-khah
pollo (chicken) = p**oh**-yoh
queso (cheese) = k**eh**-ssoh
riñon (kidney) = ree-**nyon**
solomillo (sirloin) = soh-loh-**mee**-yoh
tenedor (fork) = teh-neh-**dor**
tiburón (shark) = tee-boo-**ron**
vajillas (dishes\pots) = vah-**khee**-yass
yema (egg yolk) = (ee)-**em**-ah

Plurals

Words ending in a vowel are made plural by adding **s**:
    haba (bean), ***habas***.

Words ending in a consonant are made plural by adding **es**:
    batidor (whisk), ***batidores***.

Words ending in **z** become plural by losing the **z**, and adding **ces**:
    nuez (nut), ***nueces***.

ENGLISH \ SPANISH

INGLÉS \ ESPAÑOL

Absinthe .... ajenjo.
aged: cheese .... añejo.
      wine .... reserva.
a la carte .... combinados.
alcohol .... alcohol.
alcoholic .... alcohólico.
allspice .... pimienta inglesa\de Jamaica.
almonds .... almendras.
      sugared .... almendras garrapiñadas.
aloe .... áloe.
aluminium foil .... papel aluminio.
anchovies:
      cured .... anchoas.
      fresh .... boquerones.
angler fish .... rape.
aniseed .... anís; matalahuga.
anisette .... anís.
aperitif .... aperitivo.
appetiser .... aperitivo.
appetising .... apetitoso.
appetite .... apetito.
apple .... manzana.
      corer .... descorazonador.
      dried, cored rings .... orejones.
      pie .... tarta de manzana.
      sauce .... compota de manzana.
apricot .... albaricoque.
      dried .... orejon.
April .... abril.
apron .... delantal.
arrowroot .... arrurruz.
artichoke .... alcachofa; alcaucil.
      Jerusalem artichoke .... cotufa.
arugula (rocket) .... rucola.
asparagus .... espárragos.
      tips .... puntas\yemas de espárragos.
aspartame .... aspartamo.
aspic .... aspic; galantina.

assorted\assortment	surtido.
au gratin	gratén de; gratinado.
aubergine	berenjena.
August	agosto.
Autumn	otoño.
avocado	aguacete.
salad	guacamol.

Baby food	comida de bebe.
baby milk	leche para lactantes.
baby's bottle	biberón de bebe; tetero.
teat for	tetilla.
bacon	bacon; beicon; panceta.
and eggs	huevos con tocino.
back bacon	tocino.
slice of	torrezno.
bain marie	baño maría.
bake, to	hornear.
baker	hornero; panadero.
bakery	panadería.
baking cases	moldes de magdalenas.
baking powder	levadura en polvo.
baking soda	bicarbonato de sódico.
baking tray	bandeja para hornear; tartera.
bamboo shoots	puntas de bambú.
bananas	bananas; plátanos.
banquet	festín; banquete.
barbecue\d	barbacoa.
sauce	salsa de barbacoa.
barbecued meat	churrasco.
barley	cebada.
pearl	cebada perlada.
barrel	carril.
basil	albahaca.
bass	lubina.
baste, to	hilvanar; lardear.
batter	pasta para rebozar; fritura.
to coat with batter	rebozar.

battered	rebozado.
bayleaf	laurel.
whole bayleaves	hojas de laurel.
beans	alubias; judías; frijoles.
black eyed	judía de careta; chícharos.
broad	habas.
butter	fabas.
cut green	judías verdas cortados.
flageolet	frejoles verde.
French\green	judías; habichuela.
giant butter	garrofón; alubias granja.
haricot	pochos.
kidney	alubias riñones; pochas.
red	alubias rojas.
lima	frijol de media luna.
soya	frijol soya.
beansprouts	soja germinada; brotes de soya.
beater	batidor.
bechamel sauce	salsa bechamel.
bed of lettuce	lecho de lechuga.
beef (*see also* Introduction)	carne de vaca; vacuna.
fillet	lomo de toro.
hung	tasajo.
minced\ground	carne molida de vaca.
shoulder	espaldilla.
stew	estofado de vaca.
stock	caldo de vaca.
topside	cadero de toro.
beer	cerveza.
dark	cerveza negra.
draught	cerveza caña\de barril.
half pint (ish)	tubo.
pint	jarra.
beetroot	remolacha.
cooked	remolacha cocida.
bell pepper (capsicum)	pimiento.
belly pork	panceta.
best before	consumir preferentemente antes.

bilberry	arándano.
bill of fare	lista de platos; menú.
biologically grown	cultivo ecológico; agricultura ecológica\biologica.
biscuits	galletas; pastas.
bitter (taste)	amargo; acíbar.
black	negro.
blackberry	zarza; zarzamora.
blackcurrant	grosella.
blackeyed bean	chicharo; judía de careta.
black pudding	morcilla asturiana.
blanche, to	escaldar.
blancmange	crema de maizena.
blend	pasar por la licuadora.
to blend	batir.
blender	batidora.
blood	sangre.
sausage (black pudding)	morcilla asturiana.
blood orange	naranja sanguina.
blueberry	arándano.
boar	jabalí.
boil, to (cook food)	cocer.
boil, to (water)	hervir; bullir.
boiled	hervido.
potatoes	patatas cocida.
boiling	herviendo; ebullición.
point	punta de ebullición.
water	agua herviendo.
bone	espina; hueso.
marrow	medula.
boned	deshuesado.
borage	borraja.
bottle	botella.
feeding bottle	tetera; biberon de bebe.
opener	decapsulador; abrebotellas.
stoppers with lever	tapones de palanca.
bouillon cube	pastilla de caldo.

bouquet (of wine)	nariz.
bouquet garni	ramillettes de hierbas aromaticas.
bourbon	whiski americano.
bowl	tazon; bol; escudilla.
earthenware	gacha.
mixing bowl	tazon bol mezclas.
bowls (crockery)	cazuelitas de barro.
brace (of game)	pareja.
brains	sesos.
fried	sesada.
braise, to	brasear; rehogar.
braised	braseado.
bran	salvado; afrecho.
brandy	coñac.
brazil nut	coquito; castaña de brazil.
bread	pan.
basket	panera.
brown	pan integral.
fresh	pan tierno.
fruitloaf	pan de pasas.
gluten-free	pan sin gluten.
homemade	pan casero.
large loaf	hogaza.
loaf	barra.
roll	panecillo.
ryebread	pan de centeno.
sliced	pan rebanado.
stale	pan duro.
stick	grisín.
"tin" (mould-baked)	pan de molde; pan inglés.
tin (metal mould)	molde para pan.
uncut	sin cortar.
wholemeal	pan integral.
without crusts	sin corteza.
breadcrumbs	pan rallado.
breaded	empanado.
breakfast	desayuno.
full cooked	desayuno completo.

bream	besugo.
gilthead bream	dorada.
sea bream	globito.
breast: of bird	pechuga.
of mammal	pecho.
brine	salmuera.
brisket	falda.
broad beans	habas.
broccoli	brecól; bróculi.
broth	caldo.
brown	marrón.
bread	pan integral.
rice	arroz integral.
to brown	dorar.
Brussels sprouts	coles de bruselas.
bubbles	burbujas.
buckwheat	alforfón.
buffet	bufete; aparador.
bun	bollo; buñuelo.
bunch of fruit	gajo.
bunch of grapes	grumo de uvas.
bung\plug	taco.
burger	hamburguesa.
burgundy	burgoña.
butcher	carnicero.
butcher's shop	carnicería.
butter	mantequilla.
to butter	enmantecar.
cake	mantecado.
clarified	mantequilla fundida.
dish	mantequera.
knob of	nuez de mantequilla.
melted	mantequilla derretida.
butter beans	alubia granja.
giant butter beans	garrofón.
buttered	mantecada; untar con mantequilla.
buttermilk	suera de leche; leche de manteca.
buttery	mantecoso.

Cabbage .... col; berza; repollo.
    drumhead .... repollo liso.
    hearts .... grelos.
    red .... berza lombarda.
    savoy .... repollo rizado.
    white .... col blanca.
    young .... collejas.
caffeine .... cafeina.
cake .... bizcocho; pastel.
    mould (loose base) .... molde desmontable.
    shop .... repostería.
calorie .... caloria.
camomile .... manzanilla; camomila.
can (tin) .... lata.
    opener .... abrelatas.
candied .... garrapiñado.
candy (sweets) .... confitadas; caramelos.
candyfloss .... azucarillos; algodon dulce.
candy store .... bombonería.
canned .... enlatado.
cannelloni .... canelones.
cantaloupe melon .... cantaloupo.
capers .... alcaparras.
capon .... capón.
capsicum .... pimiento; aji; cápsico.
carafe .... garrafa.
    large .... garrafón.
caramel .... caramelo.
caramelise, to .... caramelizar.
caramelised .... quemada.
caraway seed .... alcaravea.
carcass .... caparazon.
cardamom .... cardamomo.
cardoon .... cardo.
Caribbean .... caribe.
carob .... algarrobo.
carp .... carpa.
carrot .... zanahoria.

carry out (takeaway)	para llevar.
carton (milk\juice)	brik.
carve, to	trinchar.
cashew nut	anacardo; marañon.
casserole	cacerola; puchero.
dish	cazuela.
round	cazuela redonda.
with lid	cazuela con tapa.
caster sugar	azúcar extrafino.
catering	provisión de alimento.
catfish	barbo.
catsup	salsa de tomate.
cauliflower	coliflor.
cayenne pepper	pimienta de cayenna.
celery	apio.
salt	sal de apio.
cereal	cereal; granos.
chamomile	manzanilla; camomila.
champagne	champan.
stopper	tapon cava.
charcoal for BBQ	carbón vegetal.
chard	acelgas.
cheese	queso.
aged	añejo; viejo.
blue	queso azul.
cottage	requeson granulado; natarón.
cow's milk	queso de vaca.
cream cheese	requeson.
cured	curada.
goat's milk	queso de cabra.
grated	queso rallado.
mature	añejo.
melted	queso fundido.
mild	queso suave.
parmesan	parmesano.
round (edam)	queso de bola.
semicured	semicurada.
sheep's milk	queso de oveja.

soft cheese	....	queso blando.
straws	....	palitos de queso.
young	....	tierno.
cheeseboard	....	bandeja de quesos.
cheeseburger	....	hamburguesa con queso.
cheesecake	....	pastel de queso; quesadilla.
cheesedish	....	quesera.
chef	....	cocinero.
cherry	....	cereza.
black	....	guinda.
chervil	....	perifollo.
chestnut	....	castaña.
dried	....	castaña pilonga.
chewing gum	....	chicle.
chicken	....	pollo.
breast	....	pechuga de pollo.
drumstick\thigh\leg	....	muslo de pollo.
farm raised	....	de corral.
free range	....	de campero.
nuggets	....	trocitos de pollo.
stock	....	caldo de pollo.
wings	....	alas de pollo.
young	....	pollita.
chickpeas	....	garbanzos.
chicory	....	achicoria.
chilled	....	enfriado.
chilli pepper	....	guindilla; ñora.
chill, to	....	enfriar.
china (crockery)	....	loza.
fine china	....	loza fino.
Chinese	....	chino.
chinese leaves	....	col chino.
chips\french fries\crisps(US)	......	patatas fritas; papas fritas; patatas francesa.
chives	....	cebollinas; ciboulettes.
chocolate	....	chocolate.
chop, to	....	picar.

25

chop	chuleta; costilla.
large	chuletón.
rib chop	costilla.
small	chuletita; chuletilla.
chopped	picado.
chopping block	tajadero.
chopping board	tabla cortar.
chunk	trozo.
cider	sidra.
cinnamon	canela.
stick	canela en rama.
ground	canela molido.
citrus fruits	citricos.
clam	almeja; escupiña.
claret	clarete.
clean	limpio.
to clean	limpiar.
clear	claro.
cleaver	cuchilla grande.
clementine	clementina.
clingfilm	plástico para envolver.
clove	clavo (de comer\olor).
of garlic	diente de ajo.
cloying	empalagoso.
coaster	portavasos.
cochineal	cochinilla.
cockles	coquines; berberechos.
cocktail	cóctel; combinado.
shaker	coctelera.
stick	palillo.
cocoa	cacao.
butter	manteca de cacao.
powder	cacao en polvo.
skimmed cocoa powder	cacao desgrado en polvo.
coconut	coco.
cod	bacalao.
coffee	café.
black	café solo\negro.

black with brandy	café carajillo.
black & weak	café americano.
decaffeinated	café descafeinado.
espresso	café exprés.
iced	café con hielo.
iced, black	café solo con hielo.
large in a glass	(choice) vaso grande.
instant	café instantáneo.
large	grande; doblo.
percolator	cafetera de filtro.
pot	cafetera.
milky weak	café manchada.
with little milk	café cortado.
strong	cargado.
50\50 milk	café con leche.
cognac	coñac.
colander	coladera; coladór.
cold	fria\frio.
cold meats	fiambre.
mixed	embutidos mixtos.
coleslaw	ensalada de col.
coley	carbonero.
coltsfoot	fárfara.
comfrey	sínfito.
condensed milk	leche condesada.
condiment	condimento.
confectionery	confitería; repostería.
conger eel	congrio.
consommé	caldo.
container	recipiente.
contents	contenido.
cook	cuece.
person (chef)	cocinero.
to cook	cocer; cocinar; guisar.
cookbook	recetario; libro de cocina\cocinar.
cooked	cocido.
cookery	cocina.
cookies	galletas.

cooking	cocimiento; cocción.
pot	marmita.
cool	fresco.
to cool	refrigerar; refrescar; entibiar.
cooling rack	rejilla.
copper	cobre.
copperware	objetos de cobre.
coriander	cilantro.
cork	corcho.
corkscrew	sacacorchos; tirabuzon.
corn	maiz.
cornflour\cornstarch	harina de maiz; maicena.
oil	aceite de maiz.
on the cob	maíz en mazorca.
sweetcorn	maiz dulce.
corncob	corazón de mazorca; panoja.
baby corncobs	mazorquitas.
cornflakes	copos de maiz tostados.
cornflour	harina de maiz; maicena.
cottage cheese	requeson granulado; natarón.
cotton candy (candyfloss)	azucarillos; algodon dulce.
courgette	calabacin; calabacita.
course	plato.
first course	primer plato; 1° plato.
second\main course	segundo plato; 2° plato.
cover (lid)	tapa; cobertera.
cover, to	cubrir; tapar.
cover charge	precio del cubierto.
cow	vaca.
crab	cangrejo; buey del mar.
meat	carne de cangrejo.
spidercrab	centolla.
crabapple	manzana silvestre.
crabsticks	tronquitos de mar.
cracker	galleta salada.
crackling	piel crujiente de cerdo; pedacitos de carne.
cranberry	arándo agrio; arandano.

crayfish	langosta; langostin; cigala; cangrejo de rio.
cream (general)	crema.
to cream	batir.
cream (of milk)	nata.
double	nata enriquecida.
for cooking	nata para cocinar.
for whipping	nata para montar.
single	nata liquida.
whipped	nata montada.
cream cheese	requeson.
cream of tartar	tártaro
creamy	cremoso.
crépe	crespón.
cress	berro de jardín.
crisps	patatas fritas.
crispy	crespo; crujiente.
crockery	loza; cacharros.
croquette	croqueta.
croûtons	picatostes; migas (de pan).
cruet	ampolla.
crumble, to	desmenuzar.
crumbled	desmenuzado.
crunchy	crujiente.
crushed	machachado.
crush, to	estrujar.
crust	corteza; costra.
crusty	crujiente.
cubed	dados.
cubes	cubitos; cubos.
cucumber	pepino; cohombro.
long (UK familiar)	pepino Hollandes.
short	pepino blanco.
culinary	culinario.
cumin	comino.
cup: for tea	taza.
for wine	copa.
cup of tea	taza de té.

curd\junket	cuajada.
curdle, to	cuajar.
cured	curada.
ham	jamón serrano.
curly	rizado.
currants	pasas\uvas de Corinto.
curry	curri.
custard	natillas.
egg custard	natillas de huevo.
tart	flan.
custard apple	chirimoya.
cut	cortado.
in half	cortar en mitades.
to cut	cortar.
cut green beans	judías verdas cortados.
cutlery	cubiertos; cuchillería.
case	posada.
cutlet	chuletilla; chuleta.
cuttlefish	jibia; sepia.
small	chopito.

Dairy	lechería.
products	derivados lácteos.
non-dairy	no lechero.
damson	ciruela damascena.
dandelion	diente de leon; amargón.
Danish	danés.
dash (a dash of)	chorrito de.
date: fruit	dátil.
time	fecha.
out of date	antecuado.
decaffeinated	descafeinado.
decanter	garrafa.
decant, to	decantar.
December	diciembre.
deep	hondo.
freeze	congelador.

deer	ciervo.
defrost	descongelar.
defrosted	descongelado.
delicatessen	fiambrería.
demijohn	botellón.
de-scale, to (fish)	escamar.
de-seed, to	desgranar.
dessert	postre.
spoon	cuchara de postre.
dextrose	dextrosa.
diced	en dados.
diet	dieta; regimén especial.
to diet	adelgazar.
dill (herb)	eneldo; hediondo.
dill pickles	pepinillos.
dilute, to	diluir; desleir.
dine, to	cenar.
dining room	comedor.
dining table	mesa de comedor.
dinner	cena.
party	veláda.
dish (crockery):	
deep	plato hondo.
large	fuente.
dish (meal)	plato.
dishcloth	bayeta; fregador.
dishes (pots & pans)	vajillas.
dishwasher	fregadora.
dissolve, to	desleír.
dollop of	plaston de.
donut	rosquilla; frito.
double cream	nata enriquecida.
dough	amasijo; masa.
doughnut	rosquilla; frito.
doughy	pastoso.
dozen	docena.
dress, to (a meal)	condimentar.
dress code	código de vestuario.

dressed:
    prepared (as crab) .... preparado.
    with condiment .... condimento.
dressing .... aliño; condimento.
dried fruit .... pasa.
drink .... bebida.
    large drink .... doble.
drinkable .... potable.
drinking straw .... canutillo; paja (para tomar).
drinking water .... agua potable.
dripping .... manteca; pringue; unto.
drumstick .... muslo.
dry (general and wine) .... sec; seca; seco.
duck .... pato.
duckling .... patitos.
dummy\pacifier .... chupete.
dumpling .... ñoqui.

Earthenware .... loza de barro.
    bowl .... cazuelita de barro.
eat, to .... comer.
ecological .... ecológico.
edible .... comestible; comible.
eels .... anguilas.
    baby .... angulas.
egg(s) .... huevo(s).
    barnyard .... huevo de corral.
    beaten .... huevo batido.
    cup .... huevera.
    custard .... natillas de huevo.
    devilled .... huevo ruso.
    Easter .... huevo de Pascuas.
    free range .... huevo de campero.
    fried .... huevo estrellado.
    hard boiled .... huevo duro\cocido.
    poached .... huevo escalfado.
    quail's .... huevo de cordoniz.
    scrambled .... huevos revueltos; revoltijo de huevos.

shell	cascarón.
soft boiled	huevos pasados por agua.
timer	reloj de arena.
white	clara.
yolk	yema.
eggplant (aubergine)	berenjena.
egg timer	reloj de arena.
electrical	eléctrico.
electric cooker	cocina de electricidad.
empty, to (remove contents)	vaciar.
empty, to (pour)	verter.
empty (no contents)	vacio.
en croute	en costra de.
endives	endivias.
English	inglés.
eucalyptus	eucalipto.
evaporated	evaporado.
expiry date	fecha de caducidad.
extra helping	suplemento.

Fat (lard)	unto.
fava bean	haba.
February	febrero.
fennel	hinojo; caña reja.
ferment, to	fermentar.
festival	festín.
figs	higos; brevas.
dried	higos secos.
filbert	avellana.
filet mignon	filete de solomillo.
fill, to (stuff)	rellenar.
filleted	deshuesado.
fillet steak	solomillo; tournedo.
filter, to	colar.
filter	filtro.
fine	fino.
china	loza fino.
finger	dedo.

firelighters	pastillas encendido.
first course	1°\primer plato.
fish (all)	pescado (dead); pez (alive).
caught	extractiva.
farmed	acuicultura; de crianza.
fingers	varitas de (fish type).
kebab	brocheta de pescado.
monger	pescador.
shop	pescadería.
slice	faleta pescado; paleta.
stock	caldo de pescado.
flageolet beans	frejoles verde.
flaked	desmenuzado.
flaky pastry	hojaldre.
made of f.p.	hojaldrado.
flambé	flameandos.
flame	llama; fuego.
flatware (cutlery)	cubiertos.
flavour	sabor.
flavour enhancer (MSG)	potenciador del sabor.
flavourings	aromas.
flaxseed	linaza.
flesh (pulp)	pulpa.
floret	ramita.
flounder	platija; lenguado.
flour	harina.
cornflour	harina de maiz.
dredger	tamiz.
for pastry	(para) repostería.
rice	harina de arroz.
rye	harina de centeno.
self raising	harina con levadura.
wheat	harina de trigo.
fondants	yemas.
food	comida; alimento.
cover (wire)	alambrera.
mixer	mezcladora.
wrap	plástico para envolver.

forcing bags	mangas para repostería.
fork	tenedor.
formula (baby milk)	leche para lactantes.
fowl	gallina; ave.
free range	de campero.
freezer	congelador.
freeze, to	congelar; helar.
French	francésa.
beans	judías; habichuelas.
green beans	judías verdes.
french fries	patatas fritas; papas fritas.
fresh	fresca.
fricassee	fricasé.
fridge	nevera; frigorifico.
fried	frito; fritas.
food	fritura.
in batter	rebozadas.
fries\chips	patatas fritas.
fritters	fritas; tortillitas; frisuelo.
frog (edible)	rana común.
frog's legs	ancas de rana.
frosting (icing)	alcorza.
frothy	espumosa.
frozen	congelado; helado.
deep frozen	ultracongelado.
fruit	fruta.
bunch of	gajo.
in season	fruta del tiempo.
knife	trinchete.
salad	macedonia de frutas.
seller	frutero.
shop	frutería.
fruitloaf	pan de pasas.
fruity	afrutado.
frying pan	sartén.
small	sarteneja.
fry, to	freir.
fry up	fritada.

fudge	dulce de azúcar.
full-up (sated)	repleto.
funnel	embudo; fonil.

Game	caza.
high	manido.
garlic	ajo.
clove of	diente de ajo.
mayonnaise	ali oli.
press	prensa ajos.
sauce	pebre.
sausage	chorizo.
(with garlic)	ajillo.
garnish	guarnición.
to garnish	aderezar; adornar.
gas	gas; butano.
bottle	bombona.
cooker\stove	cocina de gas.
gelatine	gelatina; jelatina.
genetically modified	manipulados genéticamente.
germ	germen.
German	alemána.
germinated	germinada.
gherkins	pepinillos.
giblets	menudillos.
gin	ginebra.
ginger	jengibre.
glacé fruits	escarchadas.
glass (tumbler)	vaso.
glazed	glaseado.
glucose	glucosa.
gluten	gluten.
goat	cabra.
young (kid)	cabrita.
goat's milk	leche de cabra.
goose	gansa; oca.
gooseberry	uva espina; grosella blanca.

grain	grano.
grammes	gramos.
grape	uva.
bunch of grapes	grumo de uvas
juice	zumo de uvas; mosto.
grapefruit	pomelo; toronja.
grate, to	rallar.
grated	rallado.
cheese	queso rallado.
grater	rallador.
gravy	grevi; salsa.
boat	salsera.
grease	grasa; pringue.
to grease	untar.
greaseproof paper	papel vegetal.
greasy	pringoso.
green	verde.
green beans	judías verdas.
cut	judías verdas cortados.
greengage	ciruela claudia.
greengrocer	verdulero.
greens	verduras.
griddle	parilla.
griddled	a la plancha.
grill	parilla.
plate	plancha.
to grill	asar a la parilla.
grilled	parrillada; a la brasa.
grocer	abacero.
grocery	abacería; tienda de comestibles.
ground	en polvo; molido; picado.
beef	carne molida de res.
groundnut\peanut	cacahuete; cuca; aráquida; maní.
grouse	urogallo; ortega.
guava	guayaba.
guest (dinner)	comensal.
guinea fowl	pintada.

Haddock	abadejo; eglefino.
smoked	cecial.
hake	merluza.
half	medio; mitad.
halibut	halibut; fletán.
halved	en mitades.
ham	jamón.
cooked	jamón de York.
cured (dried)	jamón serrano.
hock\shank	jarrete.
shoulder	pernil.
slice of	magra.
hamper	cesta; canasta.
handmill	molinillo.
hard	duro.
hare	liebre.
hash	picadillo.
hazelnut	avellana.
head	cabeza.
health food store	herboristeria; tienda de alimentos dietéticos.
healthy	saludable.
heart	corazón.
of lettuce, etc	cogollo.
heat	fuego; calor.
heat up (reheat)	recalentar.
to heat	calentar; acalorar.
heated	calentada.
heel (bread crust)	corteza, costra.
hen	gallina.
herb shop\herbalist	herbolario.
herbs	hierbas.
herring	arenque.
high (of game)	manido.
hindquarters	cuarto trasero; ancas.
homemade	casero; hecho en casa.
honey	miel.
honeycomb	panal.

honeydew melon	melon oro\amarillo.
honeyed	meloso.
hors-d'œuvre	entremeses.
horseradish	rábano picante.
hot (temperature)	caliente.
hot (piquant)	picante.
house wine	vino de la casa.
hundreds and thousands	fideos arco iris.
hungry	hambriento.
husk	cáscara.

Ice   hielo.
    cubes   cubitos de hielos.
icebox   nevera; frigorifico.
ice cream   helado; mantecado.
    cone   barquillo; cucurucho.
    parlour   heladeria.
    scoop   cuchara bola helado.
ice cube tray   bandeja de cubitos de hielo.
iced: sweet coating   glaseado.
    chilled   enfriado; con hielo (with ice).
icing   alcorza.
    bags   mangas para repostería.
    sugar   azúcar glacé\de glaseado.
    syringe   jeringa para repostería.
Indian   indio.
infusion   tisana.
ingredients   ingredientes.
inkfish   chiparóne.
invitation   convite.
invite for a drink, to   propinar.

Jam   confitura; conserva.
January   enero.
Japanese   japónes.
jar   vasija; jarra.
jellied   gelatinoso.
jello   jalea; gelatina.

jelly	jalea; gelatina.
jam (US)	confitura; conserva.
jerked beef	tasajo.
Jerusalem artichoke	cotufa.
Jewish	judío.
John Dory	San Pedro; gallo.
joint of meat	redondo de carne.
jug	jarra; cántaro.
large	jarrón.
juice	zumo; jugo.
extractor	exprimador.
juicy	jugoso; zumoso.
julienne	juliana.
July	julio.
June	junio.
junket	cuajada (de leche).

Kebab (the spike)	broqueta.
kebabs	pinchos morunos.
ketchup	salsa de tomate.
kettle	hervidor.
(pot)	marmita.
(teapot)	tetera.
kidney	riñon.
kidney bean	alubia riñon; habichuela.
red	alubia roja.
kipper	arenque ahumado.
kitchen	cocina.
foil	papel aluminio.
paper	papel de cocina.
kiwi fruit	kiwi.
knead	amasar.
kneading	amasijo.
knife	cuchillo.
blade	hoja de cuchilla.
large	cuchilla.
serrated	cuchillo dentado.

sharp	....	cuchillo afilado.
sharpener	....	afilador; chaira.
knob of butter	....	nuez de mantequilla.
kosher	....	kosher; a la judío.

Ladle	....	cacillo; cazo; cucharón; cazo cocina.
lager	....	cerveza rubio.
lamb	....	cordero.
chops	....	chuletas de cordero.
leg of	....	pierna de cordero.
shoulder of	....	paleta de cordero.
suckling	....	cochifrito.
young	....	lechon.
lard	....	manteca (de cerdo); unto.
larder	....	despensa; reposte.
lasagna	....	lasaña.
lavender	....	espliego; lavándulo.
leaf	....	hoja.
lean: little fat	....	chupado.
thin	....	magro.
leek	....	puerro.
leftovers	....	resto.
leg	....	pierna; pata.
lemon	....	limón.
zester	....	raspador limón.
lemonade	....	limonada; linoyada.
lemon sole	....	limanda; mendolimón.
lemon verbena	....	hierba luisa.
lentils	....	lentejas.
lettuce	....	lechuga.
bed of	....	lecho de lechuga.
cos	....	lechuga de romero.
curly	....	rizado.
heart	....	cogollo.
iceberg	....	iceberg.
round	....	lechuga trocadero.
licorice	....	regaliz.
lid	....	cobertera; tapa.

light: low fat	ligero.
of shade	claro.
to ignite	encender.
lighter (igniter)	encendedor.
lima bean	frijol de media luna.
lime	lima.
linseed	linaza.
liqueurs	licores.
liquid	líquido.
liquidised	triturado.
liquidise, to	liquidar; triturar.
liquorice	regaliz.
lite (low fat)	ligero.
litre	litro.
liver	hígado.
loaf (French stick)	barra. (*see also* bread)
lobster	langosta; bogavante.
loin	lomo.
lollipop	chupete.
low	bajo.
calorie	de pocas calorías.
fat (light)	ligera.
in	bajo en.
lukewarm	tibio.
lunch	almuerzo.
packed lunch	fiambrera.
to have lunch	almorzar.
lunchbox	fiambrera.

Macaroni	macarrones.
macaroon	macarrón.
mace	macis.
mackerel	caballa.
madeleines	magdalenas.
main course	2 °\segundo plato; plato fuerte.
malt	malta.
mange tout	tirabeques.
March	marzo.

margarine	margarina.
marinade	adobo.
to marinade	adobar.
marinaded	adobado; aliñada; adobo.
marjoram	mejorana.
market	mercado.
marmalade	mermelada.
marrow (vegetable)	calabacin.
marrow (of bone)	tuétano.
marrowbone	caña de vaca; hueso con tuétano.
marshmallow	malva.
marzipan	mazapán.
mashed	puré.
mashed potato	puré de patatas.
dried	puré de patatas en polvo.
matches	fósforos; cerillas (wax).
safety matches	fosforos de seguridad.
mature	maduro; curada\añejo (cheese).
May	mayo.
mayonnaise	mayonesa; mahonesa.
mead	meloja; hidromiel.
meals	platos; comidas.
measuring jug	jarra medida\medidora.
meat(all)	carne.
barbecued	churrasco.
cold	fiambre.
crabmeat	carne de cangrejo.
dried	carne seco.
smoked-dried	cecina.
meatballs	albóndigas.
medium	medio.
sweet	semidulce.
melon	melón.
baller	vaciador fruta.
canteloupe	cantaloupo; galia.
galia	galia; cantaloupo.
honeydew	melón amarillo\oro.
watermelon	sandía.

melt	derrito.
to melt	derretir.
melted	derritida; fundido.
menu (of the day)	menú (del día); la carta.
house menu	menú de la casa.
meringue	merengue.
microwave oven	microondas.
milk	leche.
baby milk.	leche para lactantes.
carton	cartón de la leche; brik.
condensed	leche condensada.
cow's	leche de vaca.
evaporated	leche evaporada.
goat's	leche de cabra.
jug	lecherita.
pasteurised	leche pasterizada.
powdered	leche en polvo.
shake	batido de ... (flavour).
sheep's	leche de oveja.
semi skimmed	leche semidesnatada.
skimmed	leche desnatada.
UHT	leche uperizada.
milkman	lechero.
milky	lechoso.
milled	molido.
millet	mijol.
mince	carne picada; picadillo.
to mince	picar.
minced	picado; picadillo de (meat type).
mint	menta; hierbabuena.
mixed	mixta; variados.
grill	frito mixtos; parrillada.
with	junto con.
mixing bowl	tazón bol mezclas.
mix, to	combinar.
mixture	mezcla.
molasses	melaza.
monkfish	rape; angelote.

monosodium glutamate	potenciador del sabor.
mortar	mortero.
and pestle	mano de almirez.
mould (shape)	molde.
ring mould	molde de anillo.
with loose base	molde desmontable.
muffin	panecillo.
mulberry	morera.
mulled wine	clarea.
mullet	mújol; calluga.
grey	lisa.
red	salmonete.
mung beans	soja verde.
mushroom	champiñón; seta.
button	champiñón pequeño.
cep	boleto.
cultivated	champiñón.
sliced	champiñón laminado.
wild	níscalo; róvellon; hongo.
mussels	mejillones.
must (fermenting grape juice)	mosto.
mustard	mostaza.
mutton	carne de carnero\cordero.
Napkin	servilleta.
ring	servilletero.
neck	cuello; pescuezo.
nectarine	nectarina; melocotón.
non-dairy	no lechero.
noodles	nidos; tallarines.
fine	fideos.
nougat *(see also* Introduction*)*	turrón .
November	noviembre.
nut\nuts	nuez\nueces (all).
on packet foods as	frutas secas.
almond	almendra.
brazil nut	castaña de brazil; coquito.

continued / seguido

nut/nuts (*continued / seguido*)
    cashew nut .... anacardo; marañon.
    filbert .... avellana.
    groundnut .... cacahuete; cuca; aráquida; maní.
    hazelnut .... avellana.
    peanut .... cacahuete; cuca; aráquida; maní.
    pecan .... pacana.
    pine nuts .... piñones.
    tiger nut .... chufa.
    walnuts .... nueces california.
nutcracker .... cascanueces.
nutmeg .... nuez moscada.

Oat .... avena.
    flakes (porridge) .... copos de avena.
oatcake .... torta de avena.
oatmeal .... harina de avena; cuáquer.
October .... octubre.
octopus .... pulpo.
    baby .... pulpitos.
offal .... desperdicios; menudillas.
oil .... aceite.
    for frying .... para freir.
    mixed seed .... aceite de semillas.
    olive .... aceite de oliva.
    rape seed .... aceite de colza.
    sunflower .... aceite de girasol.
    vegetable .... aceite vegetal.
oily .... oleoso.
olive oil .... aceite de oliva.
olives .... aceitunas.
    black .... aceitunas negra.
    green .... aceitunas verde.
    pitted\stoned .... aceitunas sin hueso.
    stuffed .... aceitunas rellenado\relleno.
    unstoned .... aceitunas con hueso.
omelette .... omelet; tortilla.
    egg only .... tortilla francesa.

onion	cebolla.
rings	aros de cebolla.
silverskin	cebolla tierna.
string of	horca; ristra.
on the rocks	con hielo.
open	abierto.
to open	abrir.
opener	abridor.
optional	potestativo.
orange	naranja.
blood orange	naranja sanguina.
juice	zumo de naranja.
mandarin	mandarinas.
segment	gajo.
sweet	de\para postre.
oregano	orégano.
organic	orgánico.
farming	agricultura biologica\ecologica; cultivo ecologico.
ostrich	avestruz.
out of date	anticuado.
oven	horno.
baked	al horno.
gloves	guantes para horno.
microwave	microondas.
proof	puedan ir al horno.
overcook, to	requemar.
overcooked\overdone	demasiado hecho.
overripe	pocho.
ox tail soup	sopa de rabo de buey.
ox tongue	lengua de buey.
oyster	ostra; ostion.
fork	desbullador.
Pacifier\dummy	chupete.
packed lunch	fiambrera.
packet	sobre.

pan	....	cazuela; cacerola.
	lid	cobertera; tapa.
	set of pans	bateria.
	small	cazo; cacito.
pancake	....	panqueque; hojuela.
pantry	....	despensa.
paper	....	papel.
	greaseproof	papel vegetal.
	kitchen	papel de cocina.
paprika	....	pimentón; pimiento colorado; pimiento húngaro.
parboil	....	sancochar.
parsley	....	perejil.
parsnip	....	chirivía; pastinaca.
partridge	....	perdiz.
party	....	fiesta; convite.
pasta	....	pasta (alimenticia).
	spirals	caracolas de pasta.
paste	....	pasta.
pasteurised	....	pasterizada.
pastry	....	pasta.
	brush	pincel de cocina.
	cases	moldes de magdalenas.
	cutters	cortapastas.
	duster	tamiz.
	flaky\puff	hojaldre.
pasty	....	pastel; empanada.
	large	empanada.
	small	empanadilla.
paté	....	paté.
pawpaw	....	papaya.
peach	....	melocotón.
	dried	orejon.
peanut\groundnut		cacahuete; cuca; aráquida; maní.
pear	....	pera.
	jam	perada.
	small	perilla.
pearl barley	....	cebada perlada.

48

peas	guisantes.
split	guisantes mondadas.
pecan	pacana.
pectin	pectina.
peel: of fruit	hollejo.
skin	piel.
to peel	pelar; descortezar.
peeled	pelado; mondada.
peeler	pelador.
pepper (peppercorns)	pimienta.
mill	molinillo.
red	pimienta rosa.
shaker	pimentero.
pepper (capsicum)	pimiento.
chilli	guindilla.
green	pimiento verde.
hot	pimiento de cometilla.
red	pimiento rojo\morron.
sweet	pimiento morrón.
peppermint	menta.
perch	perca.
percolator	percolador; cafetera de filtro.
per head	por cabeza.
periwinkle	vincapervinca; bígaro.
persimmon	caqui; kaki; sharon.
pestle	majadero.
and mortar	mano de almirez.
pheasant	faisán.
pickled	escabechadas.
pickles	encurtidos.
pickle, to	adobar; encurtir.
picnic	jira; campestre merienda.
hamper	cesta.
pie	empanada.
fruit	pastel.
small	empanadilla.
piece of	pieza\porcion de.

pig	....	cerdo; puerco.
fattened	....	de matanza.
suckling\piglet	....	lechón; cochinillo.
pigeon	....	pichon; paloma.
piglet	....	porcino; lechón.
pig's trotters	....	manos de cerdo.
pilot light	....	llama piloto.
pinafore	....	delantal.
pineapple	....	piña.
rings	....	piña en rodajas.
chunks	....	piña en trozos.
pine nuts	....	piñones.
pip	....	pepita; hueso.
pistachio	....	pistacho.
pitcher (jug)	....	jarra; cántaro.
place mat	....	salvamantel.
plaice	....	platija; acedía.
plate (crockery)	....	plato; platillo.
deep plate	....	plato hondo.
dinner plate	....	fuente redonda.
large plate	....	plato fuente.
side plate	....	plato postre.
small dinner plate	....	plato llano.
soup plate	....	sopero.
pluck, to	....	desplumar.
plug\bung	....	taco.
plum	....	ciruela.
poach, to	....	escalfar.
pod	....	vaina.
pollack	....	abadejo.
pomegranate	....	granada.
pop (fizzy lemonade)	....	gaseosa.
popcorn	....	palomitas (de maiz).
poppy	....	amapola.
seeds	....	semillas de amapola.
pork	....	cerdo; chancho.
belly pork	....	panceta.
fillet	....	solomillo de cerdo.

    loin .... lomo de cerdo.
    minced .... picada de cerdo.
    salt pork .... tocino.
    sausage .... longaniza; mortadela.
    scratchings .... chicarones.
    shoulder, salted .... lacon.
porridge .... avenate; puches; gachas.
port (wine) .... oporto.
portion .... porción; pieza.
pot   .... pote.
potato(es) .... patata; papa.
    boiled .... patatas cocida.
    chips(US) crisps(UK) ...... patatas fritas.
    jacket .... patata asada no pelada.
    mashed .... puré de patatas.
    peeler .... pela de patatas.
    roast .... patatas asada.
    salad .... ensalada patata.
    sweet potato .... batata; boniato.
potholders (oven gloves) .... guantes para horno.
potroast .... cacerola.
pots&pans\dishes .... vajillas.
poultry .... aves de corral; volatería.
    shop .... gallinería.
pour, to .... verter; echar.
    a little at a time .... instilar.
    over the top .... verter encima.
powder .... polvo.
powdered\ground .... en polvo.
prawns .... langostinos; gambas.
    baby .... camarones.
    Dublin Bay .... cigalas.
    large .... langostinas.
    very large crimson .... carabineros.
precooked .... precocido; preparado.
prepare, to .... preparar.
prepared .... preparado; listo.
preserves .... conservas; compotas.

pressure cooker	olla presión.
safety valve	válvula de seguridad.
rubber ring	anillo de goma.
pretzel	galleta torcida.
prickly pear	chumbo; higo chumbo.
propane	propano.
prune	ciruela pasa; pruna.
pudding	pudín; budín; postre.
puffed	inflado.
rice	arroz inflado.
wheat	trigo inflado.
puff pastry	hojaldre.
made of	hojaldrado.
pullet	picantón; pollastra.
pulp	pulpa.
pulses	legumbres secas.
pumpkin	calabaza.
punch	ponche.
bowl of punch	ponchada.
purée	puré.
maker	pasapure.
purple	morado.

Quail	codorniz.
quarter	cuarto.
quince	membrillo.

Rabbit	conejo.
radish	rabanito; rábano.
ragout	estofado.
rainbow trout	trucha arco iris.
raisins	uvas pasas.
ramekin	flanero.
rape	colza.
seed oil	aceite de colza.
rare (undercooked)	poco hecho.
rasher	lonja; magro.
of bacon	torrezno.

raspberry	frambuesa.
ratatouille	pisto.
raw	crudo.
razor shellfish	navaja.
ready	listo.
to eat	listo a comer.
rear (hind part)	traseros.
recipe	receta.
book	recetario.
red	rojo.
red cabbage	berza lombarda.
redcurrant	grosella.
red mullet	salmonete.
red snapper	rosada.
reduce, to	reducir; diluir.
red wine	vino tinto.
refill, to	reenvasar.
refill	recambio.
refined	refinado.
refrigerator	frigorifico; nevera.
rennet	cuaja.
restaurant	restaurante.
rhubarb	ruibarbo.
rib\rib chop	costilla.
rice	arroz.
brown	arroz integral.
flour	harina de arroz.
long grain	arroz (de grano) largo.
parboiled	arroz vaporizado.
precooked	arroz vaporizado.
pudding	arroz con leche.
round grain	arroz redondo.
short grain	arroz de grano corto.
wild	arroz salvaje.
rind	corteza.
ring (burner on cooker)	quemador; aro; arito.
ring mould	molde de anillo.
rinsed	aguajado.

ripe	maduro.
ripen, to	sazonar.
roast, to	asar.
lightly	soasar.
roasted	asado.
spitroasted	asador.
roasting dish, deep	fuente asado.
roast suckling pig	tostón.
rocket	rucola.
roe	hueva.
roll (bread)	panecillo; montadito.
filled	bocadillo.
rolling pin	palote; rodillo.
room temperature	tiempo.
rosemary	romero.
rubber	goma.
grommet	ojal.
rum	ron.
and coke	cubalibre.
rump steak	solomillo.
runner beans	judías verdas.
rusks	sequillos.
rye	centeno.
ryebread	pan de centeno.

Saccharine	sacarina.
sachet	bolsita; sobre.
sack lunch	fiambrera.
safety matches	fosforos de seguridad.
saffron	azafrán.
sage	salvia.
sago	sagu.
salad	ensalada.
avocado salad	guacamol.
bar	bar de ensalada.
bowl	ensaladera.
green salad	ensalada verde.
mixed salad	ensalada mixta.

potato salad	ensalada patata.
russian salad	ensalada ruso.
seafood salad	ensalada de marisco.
spinner	centrifugadora.
vegetable salad	ensaladilla.
salami	chorizo.
salmon	salmón.
salt	sal.
cellar\shaker	salero.
sea salt	sal marina\de mar.
salted (cured)	salazón.
salted\salty	salado.
salt pork	tocino.
salt, to	salar.
salver\tray	salva.
sandwich	bocadillo; emparedado; sandwich; sanwich.
toasted	tostada.
Saran wrap	plástico para envolver.
sardines	sardinas.
large	alachas.
small	sardinillas; sardinetas.
sarsaparilla	zarzaparrilla.
sauce	salsa.
piquant	escabeche.
saucepan	cazuela.
saucer	platillo; salsera.
sauerkraut	chukrut.
sausage	salchicha; longaniza.
large	salchichón.
sauté	saltear.
sautéed	salteado.
savoury	sabroso; salado.
scales (fish)	escamas.
scales (weighing)	balanza.
scallion (shallot)	charlota; chalote.
scallops	almejones; conchas.
scampi	cigala rebozada.

scissors	tijeras.
scone	bizcocho inglés.
scotch	whiski.
Scottish	escoches.
scouring pad	estropajo.
sea	mar.
sea bass	lubina.
seafood	mariscos.
cocktail.	salpicón de mariscos.
sea snail	caracola.
seasoning	condimento; sazonador.
season, to	sazonar; salpimentar; condimentar; salar.
seaweed	alga.
second course	segundo plato.
second helpings	suplemento.
sediment	poso.
seed	semilla; grano; pepita.
semi-skimmed	semidesnatada.
semolina	semola; sémol.
September	septiembre.
serve, to	servir.
servings	raciones.
small	tapas.
sesame	ajonjolí; sésamo.
set (hardened)	congelado.
to set	congelar.
set of pans	bateria.
set the table	poner la mesa.
settle, to (of liquids)	posar.
shake	agitar.
shallot	charlota; chalote; escaloña.
shandy	clara; cerveza con gaseosa.
shark	tiburón.
sharp	afilado.
sheep	oveja.

sheep's milk	leche de oveja.
shell, to	desvainar (peas, etc.); desbullar (oyster); desmenuzar (general); mondar (nuts and general).
shell (of crab, etc.)	caparazon.
shell (of nut, etc.)	cascarón.
shelled (nuts)	mondado.
shellfish	mariscos; moluscos.
sherry	jerez; vino de Jerez.
shop: a shop	tienda.
to shop	comprar.
shopkeeper	tendero.
shortcake	mantecada.
shoulder	brazo; paletilla; paleta.
of lamb	paleta de cordero.
shred, to	desmenuzar.
shrimps	gambas; camarones.
sieve, to	cribar.
sieve (utensil)	cedazo; tamiz; colador.
sift, to	cribar.
silver beet	acelgas.
silverware	plata labrada; vajilla de plata.
silverskin onion	cebolla tierna.
sink (basin)	fregador.
sip, to	chupar.
sirloin	solomillo; lomo bajo\alto.
skate	raya.
wings	alas de raya.
skewer	brocheta; broqueta.
skewered	en aguja; espeto.
skillet	sartén.
skimmed	desnatada.
skin	piel; hollejo.
to skin	desollar; depellejar.
skinned	pelado.

57

slice	....	loncha; lonja; rebanada.
	of bacon	torrezno.
	of cheese	loncha.
	round	rodaja.
	to slice	rebanar.
sliced	....	laminado; rebanado.
slicing machine	....	rebanador.
slotted spoon	....	espumadera.
small	....	pequeño.
	portion	tapa; dedada.
smoked	....	ahumado.
	haddock	cecial.
smooth	....	suave.
snack	....	merienda.
snail	....	caracol.
	sea snail	caracola.
soda	....	soda; sosa.
	water	agua de seltz; gaseosa.
	syphon	sifón.
sodium bicarbonate	....	bicarbonata sódico.
soft	....	blando; tierno.
	drinks	refrescos.
soften, to	....	ablandar; emblandecer.
sole	....	lenguado; acedera; platija.
	lemon sole	mendolimón.
solidified	....	congelado.
sorrel	....	acedera.
soufflé	....	suflé.
soup	....	sopa; potaje.
	ladle	cazo cocina.
	tureen	sopera.
sour	....	agrio.
soused	....	escabechadas.
soya	....	soja.
	bean	soja blanca; frijol soya.
spaghetti	....	espaguetis.
	fine	fideos.
	spoon	cuchara pasta.

sparkling	espumoso.
spatula	espátula.
spearmint	menta verde.
spice rack	especiero.
spices	especias.
spinach	espinaca.
whole leaf	hojas de espinaca.
spit	asador.
split peas	guisantes mondadas.
sponge cake	esponjos bizcochos; bizcocho.
spoon	cuchara.
dessert	cuchara de postre.
large draining	espumadera.
slotted	espumadera.
tablespoon	sopera.
teaspoon	cucharilla; cucharita.
wooden	cuchara de madera.
spoonful	cucharada.
heaped	cuchara colmados.
level	cuchara rasa.
sprat	espadin.
spread, to	untar.
sprig	ramita; pimpollo.
Spring	primavera.
spring greens	becollas.
spring onion	cebolletas; cebolla tierna.
sprinkle, to	rociar; salpicar.
sprouts	brotes.
Brussels	coles de Bruselas.
squash (pumpkin)	calabaza.
squeezed	exprimido.
squeeze, to	exprimir; estrujar.
squid	calamare; chipiróne.
baby	calamarito.
stainless steel	acero inoxidable.
stale	duro.
bread	pan duro.
starters	entradas; entremeses.

steak	filete; tajada; bistec; biftec.
fillet steak	tournedo.
medium	medio.
rare	poco hecho.
sirloin	entrecot.
tartare	bistec a la tártara.
well done	muy hecho.
steamed	cocido al vapor.
steamer	cocedor a vapor.
steel (the metal)	acero.
stainless	acero inoxidable.
steel (knife sharpener)	chaira.
steriliser	esterilizador.
sterilise, to	esterilizar.
stew	estofada; calderada; guiso; guisado.
beef stew	estofada de vaca.
to stew	estofar.
stewed	guisado; estofado.
stewpack of mixed veg	hierbas caldo; arreglo de cocido.
stewpot	olla; cazuela.
still (drink)	sin gas; sin burbujas.
stir, to	remover.
stock	caldo.
stock cube	pastilla de caldo.
beef stock cube	p.de c. de vaca.
chicken stock cube	p.de c. de pollo.
fish stock cube	p.de c. de pescado.
vegetable stock cube	p.de c. vegetal.
stoned (without stone)	sin hueso.
stones (of fruit)	huesos.
stopper	taco.
store (shop)	tienda.
store, to	guardar.
stove	estufa.
strain, to	colar.
strainer	coladera; colador.
strawberry	fresa; fresón.
straws (drinking)	canutillos; paja para tomar.

string (twine)	cuerda.
string beans	judías redondas.
cut string beans.	judías redondas troceado.
string of garlic\onions	horca; ristra.
strong	fuerte.
stuffed	rellenado; rellenas.
stuffing\filling	relleno.
stuff, to	rellenar.
sturgeon	esturión.
suckling pig	cochinillo; lechón.
roast	tostón.
suet	gordo; sebo.
sugar	azúcar.
bowl	azucarero.
brown	azúcar moreno\terciado.
cane	azúcar de caña.
caster	azúcar extrafino.
cubes	azucarillos.
demerera	azúcar morena de caña.
granulated	azúcar en polvo.
icing	azúcar glacé\de glaseado.
lump	terrón de azúcar.
syrup (sugar and water)	almíbar.
tongs	tenacillas.
sugared	garrapiñadas.
almonds	almendras garrapiñadas.
sultanas	pasas de Esmirna.
Summer	verano.
sun dry, to	charquear.
sunflower	girasol.
oil	aceite de girasol.
seeds	semillas de girasol.
supermarket	supermercado.
supper	cena.
swede	naba.
sweet	dulce; meloso.
course	postre.
overly sweet	empalagoso.

sweet and sour	agridulce.
sweetbreads	mollejas; lechecillas.
sweetcorn	maiz dulce.
sweetened	azucarado.
sweetener	edulcorante; endulzante.
sweeten, to	endulzar; azucarar.
sweet potato	boniato; batatas.
sweets	confitadas; caramelos.
sweetshop	confitería; bombonería.
swiss roll	brazo de gitano.
swordfish	pez espada; emperador.
syrup	jarabe; sirope.
cane syrup	melado.
weak as in tinned fruit	almíbar.

Table	mesa.
dining table	mesa de comedor.
tablecloth	mantel; sobremesa.
tablespoon	cuchara grande\sopera.
tableware	cubiertos.
tail	rabo.
ox tail	rabo de buey.
takeaway	para llevar.
tamarind	tamarindo.
tangerines	mandarinas.
tapioca	mandioca; mañoco.
tap water	agua corriente\del grifo.
tarragon	estragón.
tart (a cake)	torta; hornazo.
tart (taste)	agrio.
tartar	tártaro.
taste	sabor (flavour).
sense of	gusto.
to taste	gustar; catar.
to taste a little of	probar.
tasteless	desabrido; insipido.
tasty	sabroso.

tea	té.
China	té chino.
green	té verde.
teabag	bolsita de té.
teacup	taza de té.
teapot	tetera.
tearoom	salón de té.
teaspoon	cucharilla; cucharita.
teaspoonful	cucharadita.
tench	tenca.
tender	tierno.
tendon	cuerda.
tepid	tibio; templado.
testicles	criadillas.
Thai	tailandés.
thaw, to	deshelar; deshielo.
thermos flask	termos.
thick: of texture	espeso.
as slice thickness	grueso.
thighs	muslos.
thin	fino.
thirst	sed.
thousand island dressing	salsa rosa.
thyme	tomillo.
wild	figerola.
tie, to	atar.
tiger nut	chufa.
tin (can)	lata.
of	lata de.
opener	abrelatas.
tin (loaf)	pan de molde.
tinfoil	papel de estaño.
tinned	en latado; en lata.
tip (gratuity)	propina.
toast	pan tostada.
to toast	tostar.
a drink to the health of	brindis.
to drink the health of	brindar.

toasted	tostado.
toasted sandwich maker	sanwichera.
tomato	tomate.
cherry	tomate cereza.
chopped	tomate troceado.
ketchup	salsa de tomate.
paste	concentrado.
plum	tomate pera.
puréed	tomate frito.
puréed and reduced	tomate triturado.
puréed and seived	tamizado.
whole peeled	tomate entero pelado.
tongs	tenacillas; pinzas.
tongue	lengua.
ox tongue	lengua de buey.
pig's tongue	lengua de cerdo.
sheep's tongue	lengua de oveja.
tonic	tonica.
toothpicks	palillos.
topping	guarnición.
topside of beef	cadero de toro.
tough	duro.
tray	bandeja; salva.
treacle	melaza; miel de caña.
trim, to	recortar.
tripe	callos.
trivet	trébedes.
trout	trucha.
rainbow trout	trucha arco iris.
truffles (funghi)	trufas.
to stuff with	trufar.
truffles (sweet)	trufados.
tuna	atún.
salted	mojama.
tunny	atún.
turbot	rodaballo.
tureen	sopera.

turkey	pavo.
hen	pava.
turmeric	cúrcuma.
turnip	nabo; nabon de mesa.
turtle	tortuga; carey.

Unbleached (as flour) .... integral.
uncooked .... crudo.
uncork, to .... descorchar.
undercooked .... poco hecho.
unleavened .... azimo; sin levadura.
unrefined .... integral.
unripe .... inmaduro.
unsmoked .... no ahumado.
unstoned (with stone) .... con hueso.
use by .... consumir antes.

Vacuum flask .... frasco al vacio.
vanilla .... vainilla.
veal .... ternera; *(but see* Introduction*)* ternera añojo/de Avila/blanca/joven//lechal/menor.
vegetable(s) .... verdura(s); hortaliza(s); legumbre(s); vegetal(es).
    broth .... pote gallego.
    mixed vegetables .... menestra de verduras, etc.
    oil .... aceite vegetal.
    stock .... caldo vegetal.
vegetarian .... vegetariano; vegetalista.
venison .... corzo; carne de venado.
vermicelli .... fideos.
vermouth .... vermut.
vine .... vid; parra.
    leaf .... pámpana.
vinegar .... vinagre; aceto.
    bottle .... vinagrera.
vol au vent .... volovan.

Wafer .... oblea.
        cone .... cucurucho; barquillo.
waffle .... barquillo plano; gofre.
waiter .... camarero; mesero.
waitress .... camarera; mesera.
walnuts .... nueces california.
warm .... templado.
        up (re-heat) .... recalentar.
warmed .... calentada.
wash, to .... lavar.
washing up liquid .... lavavajillas.
water .... agua.
        boiling .... agua herviendo.
        cold .... agua fresca.
        drinkable .... agua potable.
        fresh .... agua dulce.
        mineral .... agua mineral.
        not for drinking .... agua no potable.
        sparkling .... agua con gas.
        spring .... agua manantial.
        still .... agua sin gas\sin burbujas.
        tap .... agua de grifo\corriente.
        warm .... agua templado.
water cress .... berro; canónigos.
watermelon .... sandía; melón de agua.
watery .... aguachirle.
wedding cake .... pan de boda.
weighing scales .... balanza cocina.
weight .... peso.
        gross .... peso bruto.
        net .... peso neto.
weigh, to .... pesar.
well done .... muy hecho.
wet .... mojado.
        to wet .... mojar.
wheat .... trigo.
        flour .... harina de trigo.
wheatgerm .... germen de trigo.

whelk	caracol de mar; búsano.
whey	suera de leche.
whipping cream	nata para montar.
whisk	batidor.
wire\balloon whisk	varillas.
white	blanco.
whitebait	chanquetes; pescado menudo.
whiting	pescadilla; merlán.
whole (complete as milk)	entero.
whole (untreated as flour)	integral.
wholemeal bread	pan integral.
wild	salvaje; silvestre.
mushrooms	níscalos.
rice	arroz salvaje.
wine	vino.
bucket	cubo para vino; balde.
cellar	bodega.
dry	vino seco.
glass for tasting	traste.
glass of	copa de vino.
grower	viñador.
house wine	vino de la casa.
red	vino tinto.
rosé	vino rosado.
savers (levered bungs)	tapones de palanca.
skin	pellejo.
sparkling	cava.
sweet	vino dulce.
taster	catavinos.
white	vino blanco.
wineglass	vaso para vino.
winelist	carta de vinos.
wing	ala.
Winter	invierno.
with	con.
without	sin.
seeds\pips\bones	sin huesos.
wood pigeon	paloma torcaz.

wrap, to	envolver.
wrasse	merlo.

Yam ..... ñame.
yeast ..... levadura.
    brewer's yeast ..... levadura de cerveza.
    dried yeast ..... levadura en polvo.
    extract ..... extracto de levadura.
    fresh yeast ..... levadura prensada.
yellow ..... amarillo.
yellow raisins\sultanas ..... pasas de Esmirna.
yoghurt ..... yogur.

Zester ..... raspador.
zuchini ..... calabacin.

ESPAÑOL \ INGLÉS

SPANISH \ENGLISH

1° plato .... first course.
2° plato .... second\main course.

Ababol .... poppy.
abacería .... grocery.
abacero .... grocer.
abadejo .... pollack; haddock.
ablandar .... soften.
abrebotellas .... bottle opener.
abrelatas .... tin opener.
abridor .... opener.
abril .... April.
abrir .... to open.
absorvida .... absorbed.
acalorar .... to heat.
acedera .... sorrel; sole.
acedía .... plaice.
aceitar .... to oil.
aceite .... oil.
    caliente .... hot oil.
    de colza .... rape seed oil.
    de girasol .... sunflower oil.
    de maiz .... corn oil.
    de oliva .... olive oil.
    de semillas .... oil from mixed seeds.
    para freir .... oil for frying.
    vegetal .... vegetable oil.
aceitunas .... olives.
    Cacereñas .... olives from Caceres.
    con hueso .... unstoned (with stone).
    negra .... black olives.
    relleno .... stuffed.
    sin hueso .... stoned (without stone).
    verde .... green olives.
acelgas .... silver beet; chard.
acero .... steel (the metal).
    inoxidable .... stainless steel.

aceto	vinegar.
achicharrar	to roast.
achicoria	chicory.
acíbar	aloes; bitter.
acuicultura	farmed (fish).
adelgazar	to diet\slim\lose weight.
aderezar	to garnish\dress.
aderezo de mesa	seasoning.
adobado	marinaded.
adobar	to pickle.
adobo	marinated.
adornar	garnish.
adórnelos	garnish them.
adquirir cuerpo	thicken.
afilado	sharp.
afilador	knife sharpener.
afrecho	bran.
afrutado	fruity (of wine).
a fuego lento	simmer; low-medium heat.
agasajo	reception; party.
agitar	shake; stir.
bien	shake well.
agosto	August.
agotar	to drain off.
agregar	add; mix in.
agregue	add.
agricultura biologica	organic farming.
agricultura ecológica	biological.
agridulce	sweet & sour.
agrio	sour; tart (of taste).
agua	water.
con gas	sparkling water.
corriente	tap water.
del grifo	tap water.
de seltz	soda water.
dulce	fresh water.
fresca	cold water.

continued / seguido

agua (*continued / seguido*)
-     hirviendo .... boiling water.
-         salada .... salted boiling water.
-     mineral .... mineral\spring water.
-     manantial .... spring water.
-     no potable .... not for drinking.
-     pie .... plonk.
-     potable .... drinkable water.
-     sin burbujas .... still (without bubbles).
-     sin gas .... still (without gas).
-     templado .... warm\tepid water.
-     tibia .... warm\lukewarm water.

aguacete .... avocado.
aguachirle .... watery.
aguajado .... rinsed.
aguamanos .... water for washing hands.
aguar .... to water down; dilute.
aguardiente .... unmatured brandy.
-     de caña .... rum.

aguja .... skewer; needlefish; garfish.
-     *meat cut* .... *see diagrams from page 166 on.*

agujallana (*meat cut*) .... *see diagrams from page 166 on.*
agujas, en .... skewered.
agujerear .... to pierce.
ahumado .... smoked.
ajada .... garlic sauce.
ajenjo .... absinthe.
aji   .... capsicum.
ajillo .... chopped\with garlic.
ajo   .... garlic.
-     blanco .... garlic & almond soup.
-     diente de ajo .... clove of garlic.
-     prensa de ajo .... garlic press.

ajonjolí .... sesame.
al   .... to the.
ala   .... wing.
-     de raya .... skate wing.

a la brasa .... charcoal grilled.

alacha	large sardine.
a la judío	kosher.
alambrera	wire food cover.
a la parrilla	grilled.
a la plancha	griddled.
albacora	tuna.
albahaca	basil.
albardilla	batter.
albaricoque	apricot.
albóndigas	meatballs.
alcachofa	artichoke.
alcaparras	capers.
alcaravea	caraway seed.
alcaucil	artichoke.
alcayota	pumpkin.
alcohol	alcohol.
alcohólico.	alcoholic.
alcorza	icing; frosting.
alcorzar	to ice\frost.
alemána	German.
aleta	small wing; fin.
meat cut	*see diagrams from page 166 on.*
alevín	fry; young fish.
alfeñicar	to candy.
alfeñique	sugar & almond oil paste.
alforfón	buckwheat.
alga	seaweed.
algarrobo	carob.
algodón dulce	candyfloss\cotton candy.
al horno	oven baked.
alimento	food.
provisión de alimento	catering.
aliñadas	marinated.
aliñar	to season.
aliño	sauce; dressing.
ali oli	garlic mayonnaise.
allulla	scone.
almacenar	store; keep.

73

almeja	clam.
fina	clam.
japonesa	short-necked clam.
almejones	scallops.
almendras	almonds.
de cacao	cocoa beans.
garapiñadas	sugared almonds.
almíbar	weak syrup in tinned fruit.
almibarar	to sweeten.
almidon	starch.
de trigo	wheat starch.
modificado	modified starch.
almirez (mano de)	pestle & mortar.
almorzar	to eat; to have lunch.
almuerzo	lunch.
áloe	aloe.
alta potencia	high power.
alto en	high in.
altramuces	lupin seeds.
alubias	beans.
granja	large butterbeans.
pochos	kidney beans.
riñones	kidney beans.
rojas	red kidney beans.
al vapor	steamed.
amapola	poppy.
amaráco	marjoram.
amargo	bitter.
amargón	dandelion.
amarillo	yellow.
amasar	knead.
amasijo	dough; kneading.
ampolla	cruet.
anacardo	cashew nut.
añada	add.
añadir	to add.
al arroz	add to the rice.

ancas	hindquarters.
de rana	frogs legs.
anchoas	anchovies (cured).
añejo	aged (cheese).
angelote	monkfish.
anguila	eel.
angulas	baby eels.
anillo	ring.
anís	anisette; aniseed.
añojo	yearling.
ánsar	goose.
antecuado	out of date.
anterior	previous.
antes	before.
de finalizar cocción	before cooking is finished.
de servir	before serving.
antiaglomerante	anticoagulant.
apagar	put out; turn off.
aparador	buffet.
apartar del fuego	remove from the heat.
aperitivo	aperitif; appetiser.
apetito	appetite.
apetitoso	appetising.
apio	celery.
sal de apio	celery salt.
aplastar	flatten; crush.
aproximadamente	approximately.
arándano	blueberry; cranberry.
arando ágrio	cranberry.
aráquida	peanut\groundnut.
arenque	herring.
ahumado	kipper.
arito\aro	cooker burner ring.
aromas	flavourings.
aritos	rings; slices.
arreglo de cocido	stewpack of mixed veg.
arrope	syrup.

arroz		rice.
	con leche	rice pudding.
	(grano) corto	short grain rice.
	(grano) largo	long grain rice.
	harina de arroz	rice flour.
	inflado	puffed rice.
	integral	brown rice.
	redondo	round grain.
	salvaje	wild rice.
	vaporizado	precooked\parboiled rice.
arrurruz		arrowroot.
arveja		pea.
asada		roasted.
asado		roast.
asador		spit; spitroasted.
asaduras		offal.
asar		to roast.
	a la parilla	to grill.
aspartamo		aspartame.
aspic		aspic.
atadito		small bundle (herbs).
atar		to tie.
	con hilo	tie with thread.
atún		tuna.
ave		fowl.
avellana		hazelnut; filbert.
avena		oat.
	copos de avena	oat flakes (porridge).
	harina de avena	oatmeal.
	torta de avena	oatcake.
avenate		porridge.
aves de corral		poultry.
avestruz		ostrich.
azafrán		saffron.
ázimo		unleavened.
azúcar		sugar.
	de caña	cane sugar.
	de glaseado	icing sugar.

en polvo	granulated.
extrafino	caster sugar.
glacé	icing sugar.
moreno	brown sugar.
morena de caña	demerara sugar.
terciado	brown sugar.
terrón de azúcar	sugar lump.
azucarado	sweetened; candied.
azucarar	to sweeten.
azucarero	sugar bowl.
azucarillos	sugar cubes; candyfloss.

Babilla *(meat cut)*	*see diagrams from page 166 on.*
bacalao	cod.
bacon	bacon.
bacoreta	little tuna.
baila	common bass.
baja potencia	low power (microwave).
baje el fuego	lower the heat.
bajo	low.
en	low in.
balanza (cocina)	weighing scales.
balde	wine bucket.
banana	banana.
bandeja	tray.
de quesos	cheeseboard.
de cubitas de hielo	ice cube tray.
para hornear	baking tray.
banderillas	small skewers for finger food
baño maría	bain marie.
banquete	banquet.
barbacoa	barbecue; barbecued.
salsa de barbacoa	barbecue sauce.
barbo	catfish.
barquichuelos	cockles.
barquillo	ice cream cone; wafer.
plano	waffle.
barra	loaf (stick).

barriga	belly.
batata	sweet potato.
bateria	set of pans.
batido de (fruit etc.)	milk shake.
batido para rebozar	batter.
batidor	whisk.
batidora	blender.
batir	to beat\blend.
el huevo	beat the egg.
baya	berry.
bayeta	dishcloth.
bebida	drink; beverage.
becacina	snipe.
becada	woodcock.
becollas	spring greens.
beicon	bacon.
bellota	acorn.
berberecho (verde)	cockle.
berenjena	aubergine; eggplant.
berro	water cress.
de jardín	cress.
berza	cabbage.
lombarda	red cabbage.
besugo	sea\red bream.
biberón de bebe	baby's bottle.
bicarbonata ammónico	ammonium bicarbonate.
bicarbonata sodico	sodium bicarbonate.
bien fria	chilled.
bife	beef.
biftec	steak.
bígaro	periwinkle.
biscottes	small, dry toasts.
biste	steak.
bistec	steak.
a la tártara	steak tartare.
bizcocho	cake; spongecake.
inglés	scone.
blanco	white.

blando	soft.
blanquillo	egg white.
blini	open\topless bap.
bocadillo	filled roll; snack.
bocadito	small cake; biscuit.
bocado	morsel.
del rey	delicacy; titbit.
bodega	wine cellar.
bogavante	lobster.
bol	bowl.
bola	ball.
boleto	wild mushroom.
boletus edulis	edible funghi.
bolito	cep mushroom.
bollo	bun; bread roll.
bolsa	bag.
bolsita	small bag; sachet.
de té	teabag.
bombonería	sweetshop; candystore.
boniato	sweet potato (red).
bonito	striped tuna.
boquerones	fresh anchovies.
borbotón	boiling vigorously.
borracho	cooked in wine.
borraja	borage.
borrego	young lamb.
bota	leather wine bag.
bote	jar.
botella	bottle.
botellón	large bottle; demijohn.
botija	earthenware jug.
botijo	drinking jar with spout.
braseado	braised.
brasear	to braise.
brazo	shoulder.
de gitano	swiss roll.
brazuelo	shoulder.
meat cut	*see diagrams from page 166 on.*

brecól	broccoli.
bren	bran.
bresca	honeycomb.
breva	fig.
brik	carton (milk\juice)
brindar	to toast the health of.
brindis	a toast to someone.
brocheta	skewer.
de pescado	fish kebab.
bróculi	broccoli.
broqueta	skewer.
brotes	buds; sprouts.
de soya	beansprouts.
brut	drier than seco.
brut de brut	drier than brut (of cava).
buche	crop; gizzard; belly.
budín	pudding (can be savoury).
buey	bullock; ox.
del mar	crab.
bufete	buffet.
bullir	to boil (water).
buñuelo	bun; doughnut; fritter.
burbujas	bubbles.
Burgoña	burgundy.
búsano	whelk.
butifarra	sausage.

Caballa	mackerel.
cabello (de angel)	fruit cut into fine threads.
cabellos	pastries filled with fruit threads.
cabeza	head.
cabeza *(meat cut)*	*see diagrams from page 166 on.*
cabra	goat.
cabrito	young goat.
cacahuete	peanut\groundnut.
cacao	cocoa.
desgrado en polvo	skimmed cocoa powder.
manteca de cacao	cocoa butter.

cacerola	saucepan; casserole; potroast.
cacharros	crockery.
cacillo	ladle.
cacito	small pan.
cadera *(meat cut)*	*see diagrams from page 166 on.*
cadero de toro	topside of beef.
café	coffee.
americano	weak black.
carajillo	black coffee & brandy.
con hielo	iced no milk.
con leche	half milk.
cortado	with little milk.
doblo\grande	large coffee.
exprés	espresso.
descafeinado	decaffeinated.
instantáneo	instant coffee.
largo	little milk.
manchada	weak; milky.
mitado	half milk.
nube	mostly milk.
soló	black espresso.
sombra	weak and milky.
vaso de	in a glass.
cafeina	caffeine.
cafetera	coffee pot.
de filtro	filter-type coffee pot.
caja	box.
cajita	small box\carton.
calabacin	courgette\zuchini; marrow.
calabacita	courgette.
calabaza	pumpkin; squash.
calabazate	sugared pumpkin.
calabazo	gourd; pumpkin.
calamar	common squid.
veteado	veined squid.
calamares en su tinta	squid in their ink.
calamarín menor	little squid.
calamarín picudo	European squid.

calamarito	baby squid.
calándolas	insert them between.
caldera	cauldron; stew.
calderada\calderetta	stew.
caldo	broth; stock; consommé.
de ave	chicken (etc.) stock.
de cocción	the cooking liquid.
de pescado	fish stock.
de ternera	beef stock.
pastilla de caldo	stock cube.
calentada	heated; warmed.
calentar	to heat.
sin hervir	heat without boiling.
caliente	hot; warm.
callos	tripe.
calluga	mullet.
calor	heat.
caloria	calorie.
camarera	waitress.
camarero	waiter.
camarón	shrimp; small prawn.
camomila	camomile\chamomile.
campero	outdoor.
campestre merienda	picnic.
caña	cane; stick; twig; rod.
de azúcar	sugar cane.
de vaca	marrow bone.
dulce	sugar cane.
reja	fennel.
canasta	hamper.
candeal	white flour.
canela	cinnamon.
en rama	cinnamon stick.
molido	ground cinnamon.
canelones	cannelloni.
cangrejo	crab\crayfish.
de rio	freshwater crayfish.
canilla	shin bone.

canónigos	water cress.
cantaloupo	canteloupe melon.
cántaro	jug; pitcher.
cantelo	celebratory bread.
cantero de pan	crust of bread.
cantidad	quantity.
canutillos	drinking straws.
capa	layer.
caparazon	shell; carcass.
capón	capon.
cápsico	capsicum; pepper.
caqui	persimmon.
carabineros	large prawns (crimson).
caracol	snail.
de mar	whelk.
caracola	sea snail.
caracolas de pasta	pasta spirals.
carajillo	black coffee & brandy.
caramelizar	to caramelise.
caramelo	caramel.
caramelos	sweets.
caráota	french bean.
carbón (vegetal)	charcoal.
carbonada	steak/chop.
carbonero	coley.
carbonizado	charred.
cardamomo	cardamom.
cardo	cardoon.
carey	turtle.
cargado	strong coffee.
caribe	Caribbean.
carne	meat.
de cangrejo	crab meat.
de carnero	mutton.
de cerdo	pork.
de cordero	lamb.
de vaca	beef.

continued / seguido

carne (*continued / seguido*)
- de venado .... venison.
- molida de res\vaca .... minced\ground beef.
- picada .... mince.
- seco .... dried meat.

carnero .... mutton.
carnicería .... butcher's shop.
carnicero .... butcher.
carnoso .... fleshy.
carpa .... carp.
carral .... wine barrel.
carralero .... cooper.
carril .... barrel.
carrillada .... pig's cheek.
carrillo .... cheek.
carta, la .... the menu.
- del vinos .... winelist.

cascanueces .... nutcracker.
cascar .... to crack.
cáscara .... shell; husk.
cascarón .... eggshell; nutshell.
cáseo .... curd.
casero .... homemade.
castaña .... chestnut.
- de brazil .... brazil nut.
- pilonga .... dried chestnut.
- regoldana .... horse chestnut.

castañero .... chestnut seller.
catar .... to taste.
catavinos .... winetaster.
cava .... sparkling wine.
caza .... game.
cazada .... ladleful.
cazo .... ladle; small pan.
- cocina .... soup ladle.

cazón .... tope; dogfish.

cazuela	casserole dish; stewpot.
con tapa	casserole dish with lid.
redonda	round casserole dish.
cazuelita	small pan; crockery bowl.
de barro	earthenware bowl.
cebada	barley.
perlada	pearl barley.
cebolla	onion.
aros de cebolla	onion rings.
escalonia	shallot\scallion.
francesa	shallot\scallion.
ristra\horca de cebolla	string of onions.
tierna	spring onion; silverskin.
cebollinos	chives.
cebollitas francesas	shallots\scallions.
cebolleta	spring onion.
cebon	fattened pig.
cecial	smoked haddock.
cecina	salted; cured; smoke-dried meat.
cedazo	sieve; strainer.
céfalo	mullet.
cena	supper; dinner.
cenar	to dine.
centeno	rye.
pan de centeno	rye bread.
centolla	spider crab.
centrifugadora	salad spinner.
cepillar	to brush.
cerdo	pork; pig.
de matanza	fattened pig (for festival).
lomo de cerdo	pork loin.
manos de cerdo	pig's trotters.
picada de cerdo	pork mince.
solomillo de cerdo	fillet of pork.
cerezas	cherries.
cerillas	wax matches.
cerner	to sift.

cerveza	beer.
caña	draught beer.
con gaseosa	shandy.
de barrill	draught beer.
jarra de cerveza	pint of beer.
negra	dark beer.
rubio	lager.
cesta	hamper.
cestito	small basket.
chabanaco	apricot.
chacina	pork sausage.
chacolí	a Basque wine.
chaira	butcher's steel (knife sharpener).
chalote	shallot\scallion.
champan	champagne.
champiñon	mushroom (cultivated).
laminado	sliced.
pequeño	button mushrooms.
chancho	pork.
chanquetes	whitebait.
charcutería	cured-meat shop.
charlotas	shallots\scallions.
charque	dried food.
charquear	to sun-dry.
chicarones	pork scratchings.
chicharo	black eye bean.
chicle	chewing gum.
chicoria	chicory.
chino	Chinese; conical sieve.
chipirón	squid; inkfish.
chirimoya	custard apple.
chiringuito	snack bar.
chirivía	parsnip.
chirla	small clam.
choco	cuttlefish.
canario	African cuttlefish.
chopa	sea bream.
chopito	small cuttlefish.

choquito (picudo)	cuttlefish.
chordón	raspberry.
chorizo	spicy (garlic) sausage; salami.
chorrito de	a dash\squirt of.
choto	unweaned animal.
chucrut	sauerkraut.
chufa	tiger nut.
chuleta	chop; cutlet.
de cordero	lamb chop.
de cerdo	pork chop.
chuletilla	cutlet; small chop.
chuletita	small chop.
chuletón	large chop.
chumbo	prickly pear.
chupado	lean (little fat).
chupar	to suck\sip.
chupete	lollipop; dummy\pacifier.
churdón	raspberry.
churra	yearling.
churrasco	barbecued meat.
churros	sweet fritters.
churrusco	toasted bread; breadcrust.
ciboulette	chives.
cidra	a squash (pumpkin).
ciervo	deer.
cigala	Dublin Bay prawn.
rebozada	scampi.
cigarra	locust lobster.
cilantro	coriander.
ciruela	plum.
claudia	greengage.
damascena	damson.
de yema	yellow plum.
pasa	prune.
citricos	citrus fruits.
citrón	lemon.
clara	egg white; shandy.
clarea	mulled wine.

clarete	claret; rosé.
claro	clear; light (shade).
claudia	greengage.
clavo (de comer\olor)	clove.
clementina	clementine.
cobertera	saucepan lid; cover.
cobertura	covering\coating.
cobre	copper.
cocción	cooking.
cocedor	oven.
a vapor	steamer.
cocer	to cook\bake\boil.
a fuego lento	simmer.
al horno	bake in an oven.
durante 10 minutos	cook for 10 minutes.
cochifrito	suckling lamb.
cochinilla	cochineal.
cochinillo	suckling pig; piglet.
cocido	cooked; boiled.
al vapor	steamed.
de cocido	boiled.
cocimiento	cooking; baking.
cocina	kitchen; cookery.
de electricidad	electric cooker.
de gas	gas cooker; stove.
libro de cocina\cocinar	cookbook.
cocinar	to cook.
cocinero	cook; chef.
coco	coconut.
cóctel	cocktail.
coctelera	cocktail shaker.
codorniz	quail.
cogollo	heart (of lettuce, etc).
cohombro	cucumber.
col	cabbage.
blanca	white cabbage.
chino	chinese leaves.
de bruselas	Brussels sprout.

coladera\colador	strainer; colander.
colar	to strain; filter.
coles de Bruselas	Brussels sprouts.
coliflor	cauliflower.
collejas	young cabbages.
colmados	heaped (spoonfuls).
colocar	to put\place.
coloquelos	put them.
colorantes	colourings.
colza	rape (seed).
combinado	cocktail.
combinados	meals a la carte.
combinar	to mix.
comedero	edible; dining room.
comediar	to divide equally.
comedor	eating; dining room.
mesa de comedor	dining table.
comensal	dinner guest.
comer	to eat.
comestible	edible.
comible	edible.
comida	food; meal.
de bebe	baby food.
poca nutritiva	junk food.
comilona	a heavy meal.
comino	cumin.
compota	preserve.
de manzana	apple sauce.
compotera	fruit dish.
con	with.
frecuencia	frequently.
hueso	unstoned (with stone).
revestimiento	covered with a lid.
coñac	cognac; brandy.
concha	scallop.
de peregrino	great scallop.
fina	clam.
condensar	thicken.

condiciones de conservación	storage conditions.
condimentar	to season\dress.
condimento	seasoning; condiment.
con hielo	with ice; iced.
conejo	rabbit.
confitadas	sweets; preserves.
confitar	to sweeten.
confite	sweetmeat.
confitería	confectionary; sweetshop.
confitero	confectioner.
confitura	jam; preserves; candied.
congelado	frozen; set.
congelador	freezer.
congelar	to freeze\set\solidify.
congrio	conger eel.
conmover	to stir.
conseguir	to achieve\obtain.
conserva	jam; tinned food; preserves.
consistencia deseada	desired consistency.
consumir	eat.
antes	eat before (date).
del fin	eat before end of (date).
preferentemente antes	best before (date)
contenido	contents.
contra: *(meat cut)*	*see diagrams from page 166 on.*
convite	invitation; party.
copa	wineglass; cup.
copo	flake.
copos de maiz tostados	cornflakes.
coquinas	cockles.
coquito	brazil nut.
corada	offal mix.
corazón	heart.
de mazorca	corncob.
corcho	cork.
cordero	lamb.
chuletas de	lamb chops.

paleta de	shoulder of lamb.
pierna de	leg of lamb.
cornero de pan	crust of bread.
corruco	cockle.
cortado	cut.
(of coffee)	with little milk.
cortapastas	pastry cutters.
cortar	to cut.
en dos	halve.
en mitades	halve.
cortarlos en cubitos	cut into cubes.
córtelas en trozos	cut them into chunks.
corteza	crust; rind.
corzo	venison.
cosecha	harvest.
costilla	rib; rib chop; cutlet.
costra	crust.
cotufa	Jerusalem artichoke.
crema	cream (not milk).
de maizena	blancmange.
cremoso	creamy.
crespo	crispy.
crespón	crépe.
criadero	fish hatchery.
criadillas	testicles.
crianza	breeding; farmed (of fish); wine aged in wooden barrels.
criba	sieve.
cribar	sift; sieve.
croqueta	croquette; meatball.
crudo	raw.
crujiente	crispy; crunchy.
cuaja	rennet.
cuajada	curd.
de leche	junket.
cuajar	to curdle.
cuajo	rennet.

cuando	when.
alcance al punto de ebullición	when it boils.
empiece de hervir	when it boils.
empiece a montar	when it begins to stiffen.
cuáquer	oatmeal.
cuarto	quarter.
trasero	hindquarters.
cubalibre	rum and coke.
cubertería	cutlery.
cubierto	cover; table service; single place setting; house\fixed-price menu.
cubiertos	cutlery; tableware; flatware.
cubitos	cubes.
de hielo	ice cubes.
cubo para vino	wine bucket.
cubos	cubes.
cubremantel	tablecloth.
cubreplatos	food cover (wire\mesh).
cubrir	to cover.
con agua	cover with water.
cuca	peanut\groundnut.
cuchara	spoon.
bola helado	ice cream scoop.
colmadas	heaped spoonful.
de madera	wooden spoon.
de postre	dessert spoon.
grande	tablespoon.
pasta	spaghetti spoon.
rasa	level spoonful.
sopera	tablespoon.
cucharada	spoonful.
cucharadita	teaspoon; teaspoonful.
cucharas colmadas	heaped spoonfuls.
cucharetear	to stir.
cucharilla	teaspoon.
cucharita	teaspoon.

cucharón	ladle.
cuchilla (grande)	large knife; cleaver.
cuchillería	cutlery; tableware.
cuchillo	knife.
dentado	serrated.
cucuruchos	cones.
cuece	cook; boil.
cuelga	bunch of fruit.
cuello	neck.
meat cut	*see diagrams from page 166 on.*
cuerda	string; tendon.
cuesco	stone of fruit.
culantro	coriander.
culinario	culinary.
cultivo biologico\ecológico	biologically grown.
cuñete	keg.
curada	cured; aged.
cúrcuma	turmeric.
curri	curry.
cuscurro	croûton; crust of bread.

Daditos de pan fritos	croûtons.
dados	cubed; diced.
damasco	damson.
dándole la vuelta	turning them.
danés	Danish.
dar la vuelta	turn\stir occasionally.
dar un hervor	boil.
dátil	date (fruit).
deberá ser	should be.
de cada uno	of each one.
de campero	free range.
decantar	to decant.
decapsulador	bottle opener.
decorar	decorate; garnish.
de crianza	farmed (of fish); aged in wooden kegs (wine).
de cuando	occasionally.

93

dedada	small portion.
dedo	finger; cube.
dejar	to leave.
cocer	leave to cook.
enfriar	leave to cool.
reposar	leave to stand.
deje	leave.
dejela cocer	leave to cook.
déjelo en maderación	leave to steep.
del	of the.
dia	of the day.
fin de	the end of.
sobre	of the packet.
delantal	apron.
delicadeza	delicacy.
de los siguientes	of the following.
demasiado hecho	overcooked.
dentón	chub mackerel.
dentro de	within; inside.
de pocas calorías	low calorie.
derivados lácteos	dairy products.
derretir	to melt\dissolve.
derritida	melted.
derrito	melt.
desabrido	tasteless; insipid.
desayuno	breakfast.
completo	full cooked breakfast.
desbullador	oyster fork.
desbullar	to shell an oyster.
descafeinado	decaffeinated.
descarnar	to remove meat from bone.
descongelado	defrosted.
descongelar	to defrost.
descorazonador	apple corer.
descorchador	corkscrew.
descorchar	to uncork.
descortezar	to peel.
descremar	to skim (cream off).

descubierta	tart; pie without a top.
descubrir	uncover.
desecar	to desiccate.
desescamar	to de-scale.
desgrado	skimmed.
desgranar	to de-seed.
deshelar	to thaw.
deshielo	thaw.
deshojar	to strip leaves off.
deshuesado	filleted; boned.
deshuesadora	fruit stoning machine.
desjugar	to extract juice from.
desleírto	dissolve; dilute.
desmenuzado	crumbled; flaked.
desmenuzar	to crumble\shell.
desmigar	to crumble.
desmoldar	remove from the mould.
desnatada	skimmed.
desnatar	to skim.
de sobremesa	post-prandial.
desollar	to skin.
despar	to take lid\cover off.
despechugar	to remove the breast.
despellejar	to skin.
despensa	pantry; larder.
despepitar	to remove the pips from.
desperdicios	offal; waste.
despiece	cutting up of meat.
desplumar	to pluck.
despojos	offal.
después	after.
despuntar	to top and tail.
destapada	pie without a lid.
destapar	to uncover.
destaponar	to uncork.
destilar	to distil.
destripar	to gut.
desunir	divide; separate.

desvainar	to shell (peas, etc.).
deszumar	to extract juice from.
de una en una	one at a time.
devolver	return; put back.
dextrosa	dextrose.
diciembre	December.
diente	tooth; fork tine.
de ajo	clove of garlic.
de leon	dandelion.
dieta	diet.
diluir	to dilute; reduce.
diluya	blend together.
disolución	dilution.
disolver	dissolve; melt.
disponemos en una fuente	(we) arrange in a dish.
distribuir	to distribute\dish out.
disuelta	dissolved.
doblar	to double\fold.
doble	large beverage; double.
docena	dozen.
dorada	gilthead bream.
dorado	golden.
dorar	to brown.
dorarse	goldened.
dosificador helado	ice-cream scoop.
dosificar	proportion ingredients.
dosis	quantity.
dulce	sweet.
de azúcar	fudge.
de membrillo	quince jelly.
dulces	confectionery; cakes.
dulcificar	to sweeten.
durante	throughout (time).
unos 5 minutos	for about 5 minutes.
dureza	hardness.
duro	hard; tough; stale.
pan duro	stale bread.

Ebullición .... boiling; bubbling up.
echar .... to pour.
ecológico .... ecological.
edulcorante .... sweetener.
edulcorar .... to sweeten.
eglefino .... haddock.
embeber .... to imbibe.
emblandecer .... to soften.
embudo .... funnel.
embutidos .... sausages (all).
      mixtos .... mixed cold cuts.
empalagoso .... cloying; oversweet.
empanada .... large pie\pasty.
empanadilla .... small pie\pasty.
empanado .... breaded.
empapar .... to soak.
emparedado .... sandwich.
emparrillar .... to grill.
emperador .... swordfish.
emulgente .... emulsifier.
en aguja .... skewered.
encendedor .... lighter (igniter).
encender .... to light; ignite.
encendido .... lit; on.
enchilada .... corn and chilli pancake.
enchilar .... to season with chillies.
en costra de .... in a crust of.
en cuando .... occasionally.
encurtido .... pickle; pickled.
encurtidos .... pickles.
encurtir .... to pickle.
en dados .... diced.
endibia\endivia .... endive.
endulzante .... sweetener.
endulzar .... to sweeten.
endurece .... harden; set.
eneldo .... dill (herb).

enero	January.
enfrascar	to bottle.
enfriado	chilled.
enfriar	to cool\refresh\chill.
engrasado	greased.
enharinar	coat with flour.
enjuagado	rinsed.
enjuagar	to rinse.
en lata	tinned.
enlatado	tinned.
en longitud	in length.
en lugar fresco\seca	in a cool\dry place.
enmantecar	to butter.
en mitades	halved.
en polvo	powdered; ground.
en rama	unprocessed; as picked.
enrarecer	to dilute\thin.
enrollar	to roll up.
ensalada	salad.
de col	coleslaw.
de marisco	seafood salad.
mixta	mixed salad.
patata	potato salad.
ruso	Russian salad.
verde	green salad.
ensaladera	salad bowl.
ensaladilla	vegetable\potato salad.
entero	whole; complete (as milk).
entibiar	to cool.
entrada	starter.
entraña	entrails.
meat cut	*see diagrams from page 166 on.*
entrantes	starters.
entrecortar	cut halfway through\in between.
entrecot	sirloin steak; loin.
entremés	appetizer.
entremeses	hors-d'œuvre; starters.
entretanto	meanwhile.

envasar	to wrap.
envase	packaging.
envase cerrado	closed container.
envinagrar	to add vinegar to.
envinar	to add wine to.
envolver	to wrap.
erizo de mar	sea urchin.
escabechadas	soused; pickled.
escabeche	sauce piquant; pickle.
escaldar	to blanche; scald.
escalfar	to poach.
escaloña	shallot\scallion.
escama	scale of fish.
escamar	to de-scale fish.
escarchadas	glacé fruits.
escarchado	frosting.
escarola	endive.
escoces	Scottish.
escudilla	bowl.
escupiña	clam.
escurra el exceso liquido	drain the excess liquid.
escurrir	to drain.
escurrirlos	drain them.
espacio de	space of (time).
espadín	sprat.
espagueti	spaghetti.
espaldilla	shoulder.
meat cut	*see diagrams from page 166 on.*
esparcir	scatter; sprinkle.
espárragos	asparagus.
espátula	spatula.
especialidad	speciality.
especiar	to add spices to.
especias	spices.
especiería	grocery.
especiero	grocer; spice rack.
espelta	spelt (wheat-like grain).
espesa y lisa	thick and smooth.

espesante	thickener.
espesar	to thicken.
espeso	thick (of texture).
espeto	skewered.
espinaca	spinach.
hojas de espinaca	whole leaf spinach.
espinas	bones.
espinazo	spine.
espinilla	shin.
espliego	lavender.
espolvorear	sprinkle.
esponjos bizcochos	sponge cake.
espumadera	large draining spoon.
espumar	to skim.
espumosa	sparkling; frothy.
esqueleto	skeleton; carcass.
estabilizante	stabiliser.
este preparado	this product.
esterilizador	steriliser.
esterilizar	to sterilise.
estirar	to roll out.
con el rodillo\palote	with a rolling pin.
estofado	stew; stewed; braised; ragout.
de vaca	beef stew.
estofarto	stew.
estornino	Spanish mackerel; cuttlefish.
estragón	tarragon.
estrelladera	egg slice; spatula.
estrellar	to fry\break apart.
estrellas	stars.
estropajo	scouring pad.
estrujar	to squeeze\crush.
estufa	stove.
esturión	sturgeon.
eucalipto	eucalyptus.
evaporado	evaporated.
evaporar	to evaporate.

exprimador\dera	juice extractor.
exprimido	squeezed.
exprimir	to squeeze.
extractiva	caught fish (not farmed).
extracto de levadura	yeast extract.
extraer la carne	extract the meat.

Faba	dried\butter bean.
fabada	bean & sausage stew.
fabricación	production.
de casera	homemade.
fabricado por	made by.
faisán	pheasant.
fajardo	vol au vent.
falda	brisket; flank.
meat cut	*see diagrams from page 166 on.*
faleta pescada	fish slice.
fañado	1 year old animal.
fárfara	coltsfoot.
febrero	February.
fecha	date (time).
de caducidad	expiry date.
fécula	starch.
de patata	potato starch.
fermentar	to ferment.
fesol	bean.
festín	banquet; festival.
fiambre	cold meat \dish; cold cut.
fiambrera	packed\sack lunch; lunchbox.
fiambrería	delicatessen.
fibra	fibre.
alimentaria	food fibre.
fideos	noodles; vermicelli.
arco iris	hundreds and thousands.
fideua	small macaroni shapes.
fiesta	festival; party.
figerola	wild thyme.

figón	"greasy spoon" café.
filete	steak; fillet.
de solomillo	filet mignon.
filtro	filter.
fino	fine.
flameandos	flambé.
flan	custard tart.
flanero	ramekin.
fletán	halibut.
fonil	funnel.
forma de lluvia	sprinkle.
forrar	to line.
el molde	line the mould.
el fondo	line the base.
fósforos	matches.
de seguridad	safety matches.
fraga	raspberry.
fragaria	strawberry.
frambuesa	raspberry.
francésa	French.
frasco	flask; bottle\jar of.
al vacio	vacuum flask.
fregador	dishcloth; sink.
fregadora	dishwasher.
fregar	to wash up\scrub.
freír	to fry.
frejoles	beans; dried beans.
verde	flageolet beans.
fresa	strawberry.
fresca	fresh.
picada	freshly chopped.
fresón	strawberry.
fria	cold.
fricandó	beef stew.
fricasé	fricassee.
frigorifico	refrigerator.

frijól		bean.
	de media luna	lima bean.
	soya	soya bean.
frio\a		cold.
frisol		kidney bean.
frisuela		fritter.
fritada		fritter; fry up.
fritas		fried; fritters.
frito		fried; doughnut.
fritos		dish of minced meats.
	mixtos	mixed grill.
	variados	mixed grill.
fritura		fritter; batter; fried food.
fructosa		fructose.
fruta		fruit.
	del tiempo	fruit in season.
frutas secas		nuts.
frutería		fruit shop.
frutero		fruit seller.
frutilla		strawberry.
fuego		heat; flame.
	bajo	low heat.
	lento	simmer; low heat.
	medio	medium simmer.
fuente		large dish.
	asado	roasting\deep dish.
	redonda	dinner plate.
fuerte		strong.
Gacha		earthenware bowl.
gachas		porridge; gruel.
gajo		bunch of fruit.
galantina		aspic.
gáleo		swordfish.
galia		galia melon.
galio		rennet.

galleta	biscuit; cookie.
salada	cracker.
torcida	pretzel.
gallina	hen; fowl.
gallinería	poultry market.
gallineta	sand piper.
gallo	cock; rooster; John Dory.
gambaros	shrimps.
gambas	prawns.
gansa	goose.
ganso	gander.
garbanzos	chickpeas.
garrafa	carafe; decanter.
garrafon	large carafe.
garrapiñado	candied; sugared.
almendras garrapiñadas	sugared almonds.
garrapiñera	ice cream freezer.
garroba	carob.
garrofón	giant butter beans.
garrón *(meat cut)*	*see diagrams from page 166 on.*
gas	gas; butano.
gaseosa	soda water; pop.
gasificantes	raising agents.
gauso del norte	eider duck.
gazpacho	vegetable soup.
gelatina	gelatine; jelly.
gelatinoso	jellied.
germen de trigo	wheatgerm.
germinada	germinated.
ginebra	gin.
girasol	sunflower.
aceite de girasol	sunflower oil.
semillas de girasol	sunflower seeds.
glaseado	glazed; iced; icing.
globito	sea bream.
glucosa	glucose.
jarabe de glucosa	glucose syrup.
gluten	gluten.

gofre	waffle.
golosina	delicacy; sweet.
goma	rubber; gum.
guar	guar gum.
gordo	suet; lard.
gramo	gramme.
granada	pomegranate.
grano	grain; cereal; seed.
grasa	grease; fat.
vegetal	vegetable fat.
hidrogenada	hydrogenated vegetable fat.
gratén de	au gratin.
gratinado	au gratin.
grelos	cabbage hearts.
grevi	gravy.
griñón	nectarine.
grisín	breadstick.
grosella	redcurrant; blackcurrant.
blanca	gooseberry.
grosura	fat; suet.
grueso	thick (of width).
grumo de leche	curd.
grumo de uvas	bunch of grapes.
grumoso	clotty.
guacamol	avocado salad.
guachinango	red snapper.
guantes	gloves.
para horno	oven gloves\potholders.
guardar	to store.
guarnición	trimmings.
guayaba	guava.
guinda	black cherry.
guindilla	hot chilli pepper.
guindillo	capsicum.
guisado	stewed.
guisantes	peas.
mondadas	split peas.
guisar	to cook.

guiso	stew; concoction.
gustar	to taste\please.
gusto	sense of taste.
gustoso	tasty.
Habas	broad beans.
habichuela	French\runner\kidney bean.
hacer	to make\do.
puré	mash.
tiras	shred; (to make strips).
hambre	hunger; appetite.
hambriento	hungry; starving.
hamburguesa	burger.
con queso	cheeseburger.
harina	flour.
con levadura	self raising flour.
de arroz	rice flour.
de avena	oatmeal.
de centeno	rye flour.
de maiz	cornflour.
de trigo	wheat flour.
(para) repostería	for pastry.
(para) rebozar	for batter.
hasta conseguir	until you obtain.
hasta que se doren	until golden.
hay	there is\are here; we have.
hebras	strands (saffron).
hecho en casa	homemade.
hediondo	dill (herb).
heladeria	ice cream parlour.
helado	ice cream; frozen.
helar	to freeze.
hender	split; slit; cleave.
herbistoria	health food shop.
herbolario	herb store; herbalist.
hervido	boiled (water).
hervidor	kettle.

herviendo\herviente	boiling.
hervir	to boil.
hidratos de carbono	carbohydrates.
hidrogenada	hydrogenated.
hidromiel	mead.
hielo	ice.
cubitos de hielo	ice cubes.
hierba	herb.
luisa	lemon verbena.
mate	Paraguayan tea.
hierbabuena	mint.
hierbas	herbs.
caldo	stewpack of mixed veg.
de monte	wild (mountain) herbs.
silvestre	wild herbs.
hígado	liver.
higo	fig.
chumbo	prickly pear.
secos	dried figs.
hilo	thread (string).
hilvanar	to baste.
hinchar	to swell\puff up.
hinojo	fennel.
hipogloso	halibut.
hogaza	large loaf.
hoja	leaf.
de cuchilla	knife blade.
de laurel	bayleaf.
hojaldrado	made of puff\flaky pastry.
hojaldre	flaky\puff pastry.
hojuela	pancake.
hollejo	skin; peel.
homogénea	thoroughly mixed.
hondo	deep.
hongos	wild mushrooms.
horca	string of onions\garlic.
horchata	drink from tiger nuts.
hornazo	Easter cake;cake; tart.

hornear	to bake.
hornero	baker.
horno	oven.
al horno	oven-baked.
hortalizas	vegetables.
hoy	today.
huerta	vegetable garden.
hueso	bone; pip; stone.
con tuétano	marrowbone.
de santo	small celebratory cake.
hueva	roe.
huevera	eggcup.
huevo(s)	egg(s).
batido	beaten egg.
campero	free range eggs.
cocido	hard boiled egg.
con tocino	bacon and eggs.
de codorniz	quail's eggs.
de corral	free range.
de Pascuas	Easter egg.
duro	hard boiled egg.
escalfados	poached eggs.
estrellado	fried egg.
natillas de huevo	egg custard.
pasado por agua	soft boiled egg.
revoltijos de huevos	scrambled eggs.
revueltos	scrambled eggs.
rusos	devilled eggs.

Incorporar	mix.
indio	Indian.
inflado	puffed\popped.
inglés	English.
ingredientes	ingredients.
inmaduro	unripe.
insertar	to insert.
insipido	insipido.
instilar	to pour a little at a time.

integral	unrefined; whole.
intercalar	arrange; place around.
introducir	insert; put into.
invierno	Winter.

Jabalí	wild boar.
jabato	young wild boar.
jalea	jelly.
jaletina	gelatine.
jamón	ham.
de York	cooked ham.
serrano	cured ham.
meat cut	*see diagrams from page 166 on.*
japónes	Japanese.
jarabe	syrup.
de fructosa	sugar syrup.
de glucosa	glucose syrup.
jarra	jar; jug.
medida\medidora	measuring jug.
jarrete	hock of ham; ham shank.
jarrón	large jug.
jelatina	gelatine.
jengibre	ginger.
jerez (vino de)	sherry.
jeringa para repostería	icing syringe.
jibia	cuttlefish.
jira	picnic.
jiste	yeast.
judías	French\runner beans.
de careta	black eye beans.
redondas	string beans.
troceado	cut string beans.
verdas cortados	cut green beans.
judío	Jewish.
jugo	juice.
jugoso	juicy.
juliana	julienne.
julio	July.

junio	June.
junto con	mixed with.
jurel	horse mackerel.
Kaki	persimmon.
kiwi	kiwi fruit.
kosher	kosher.
La carta	the menu.
lacon	salted pork shoulder.
lácteo	milky.
laminado	sliced.
laminar	to slice.
langosta	lobster; crayfish.
langostín	crayfish.
langostinos	prawns (large).
lapa	limpet.
lardear	to baste.
largueta	almond.
lasaña	lasagna.
lata	tin (can).
de	tin of.
laurel	bayleaf.
lavándulo	lavender.
lavar	wash.
lavavajillas	washing up liquid.
lechal	young animal (suckling).
lechar	to milk.
lechazo	suckling lamb.
leche	milk.
condensada	condensed milk.
crema	custard.
de cabra	goat's milk.
de manteca	buttermilk.
de oveja	sheep's milk.
de vaca	cow's milk.

desnatada	skimmed milk.
en polvo	powdered milk.
evaporado	evaporated milk.
pasterizada	pasteurised milk.
para lactantes	baby milk; formula.
semidesnatada	semi skimmed milk.
uperizada	UHT milk.
lechecillas	sweetbreads.
lechera	milch cow; milkmaid.
lechería	dairy.
lecherita	milk jug.
lechero	milkman; dairyman.
(no lechero)	non-dairy.
lecho de lechuga	bed of lettuce.
lechón	suckling pig.
lechon	young lamb.
lechona	sow.
lechoso	milky.
lechuga	lettuce.
cogollo de lechuga	lettuce heart.
de romero	cos lettuce.
iceberg	iceberg.
rizado	curly.
trocadero	round lettuce.
lecitína	lecithin.
legumbres	vegetables; pulses.
secas	dried pulses.
lengua	tongue.
de buey	ox tongue.
de cerdo	pig's tongue.
de oveja	sheep's tongue.
lenguado	sole.
lentamente	slowly\gradually.
lentejas	lentils.
leudar	to leaven.
leudarse	to rise (of bread).

levadura	yeast; baking powder.
de cerveza	brewer's yeast.
en polvo	dried yeast.
extracto de levadura	yeast extract.
prensada	fresh yeast.
licor	liquid; liquor; spirits.
licores	liqueurs.
licuadora	blender.
liebre	hare.
ligera	light; low fat.
ligeramente	lightly.
lima	lime.
limanda	lemon sole.
limón	lemon.
limonada	lemonade.
limpiar	to clean.
limpie\limpio	clean.
linaza	linseed.
linoyada	lemonade.
liquidar	to liquidise.
liquido	liquid.
lisa	grey mullet.
liso	smooth.
lista de platos	menu; bill of fare.
listo	prepared; ready.
a comer	ready to eat.
litro	litre.
llama piloto	pilot light.
llama	flame.
llana *(meat cut)*	*see diagrams from page 166 on.*
llevar	to take; carry.
llevarlo a ebullición	bring it to the boil.
lleve a ebullición	bring to the boil.
lombarda	red cabbage.
lomo	loin; back.
alto\bajo	sirloin.
de cerdo	loin of pork.
de toro	beef fillet.

	de vaca	sirloin.
	meat cut	*see diagrams from page 166 on.*
lonchas		slices (cheese, etc).
longaniza		smoked\pork sausage.
longitud		length.
longuerión		grooved razor (shellfish).
lonja		slice; strip.
lote numero\No.		batch number.
loza		crockery; china.
	de barro	earthenware.
	fino	fine china.
lubina		sea bass.

Macarón .... macaroon.
macarrones .... macaroni.
macedonia de frutas .... fruit salad.
macerar .... to soak\steep.
machacado .... crushed.
machacan juncon .... grind together (in mortar).
machacar .... to pound\grind.
machuelo .... small sardine.
macis .... mace.
maduro .... ripe; mature.
magdalenas .... madeleines.
magra .... slice; rasher.
magro .... lean\thin pork.
mahonesa .... mayonnaise.
maicena .... cornflour; cornstarch.
maiz .... corn.
    aceite de maiz .... corn oil.
    dulce .... sweetcorn.
    en mazorca .... corn on the cob.
    harina de maiz .... cornflour.
majadero .... pestle.
malta .... malt.
malva .... marshmallow.
manchego .... sheep's milk cheese.
mandarinas .... mandarin oranges; tangerines.

mandioca	tapioca.
mangas para repostería	icing (forcing) bags.
maní	peanut\groundnut.
manido	high (of game).
manipulados genéticamente	genetically modified.
manjar	food; delicacy; tidbit.
manjua	sardine.
mañoco	tapioca.
mano de almirez	pestle and mortar.
manojo	bundle; handful.
manos de cerdo	pigs' trotters.
manteca	lard; dripping.
de cacao	cocoa butter.
mantecada	buttered; shortcake.
mantecado	butter cake; ice cream.
mantecados	biscuits.
mantecoso	buttery.
mantel	tablecloth.
mantemos en ebullición	keep it boiling.
mantener en lugar seco	keep in a dry place.
mantenerlo	maintain it; keep it.
mantequera	butter dish.
mantequilla	butter.
derretida	melted butter.
fundida	clarified butter.
nuez de mantequilla	knob of butter.
untar con mantequilla	spread with butter.
manzana	apple.
compota de manzana	apple sauce.
silvestre	crabapple.
tarta de manzana	apple pie.
manzanilla	chamomile; variety of olives.
mar	sea.
marañon	cashew nut.
marcona	almond.
margarina	margarine.
marión	sturgeon.
marisco liso	scallops.

mariscos	shellfish; seafood.
marmita	cooking pot.
marón	sturgeon.
marraco	shark.
marrano	pork.
marroco	bread.
marrón	brown.
maruca	ling.
marzo	March.
masa	dough; paste; mixture.
matalahuga	aniseed.
mayo	May.
mayonesa	mayonnaise.
mazapán	marzipan.
mazorca	corn/maize.
mazorquitas	baby corncobs.
medida	measure (an amount).
medio	medium; half.
hora	half an hour.
médula	bone marrow.
mejillón	blue mussel.
mejorana	marjoram.
melado	cane syrup.
meladura	treacle.
melar	sweet; to fill with honey.
melaza	treacle; molasses.
melocotón	peach.
meloja	mead.
melón	melon.
amarillo\oro	honeydew melon.
de agua	watermelon.
meloso	sweet; honeyed.
membrillo	quince.
memela	corn pancake.
mendolimón	lemon sole.
menestra de	mix of.
menta	mint.
verde	spearmint.

ménu	menu.
del día	today's menu.
menudillos	offal.
mercado	market.
merengue	meringue.
merienda	snack; picnic.
merlán	whiting.
merlo	wrasse.
merluza	hake.
mermelada	marmalade.
mero	grouper; rock cod.
mesa	table.
de comedor	dining table.
mescla	mixture.
mesera	waitress.
mesero	waiter.
mete de nuevo	put back in; return.
meter	to put\insert.
mezcla	mixture.
mezcladora	food mixer.
mezclar	to mix.
con	stir in; mix with.
microondas	microwave oven.
miel	honey.
de caña	treacle.
mienta	mint.
mientras	while.
remueve	while stirring.
tanto	meanwhile.
migas	crumbs; croûtons.
mijo	millet.
milanesa	fried in batter.
minutos	minutes.
mitad	half.
en mitades	in halves.
por la mitad	through the centre.
mixta	mixed.
mojado	wet.

mojama	salted tuna.
mojar	to wet.
molde	mould.
de anillo	ring mould.
de magdalenas	baking case.
desmontable	cake tin with loose base.
para pan	bread tin.
molido	ground; milled.
molinillo	hand mill.
mollejas	sweetbreads.
moluscos	shellfish.
mondadas	peeled; shelled.
mondado	shelled (nuts).
mongete	bean.
montadito	small bread roll.
mora	blackberry; mulberry.
marado	purple.
morcilla asturiana	black pudding.
morcilla blanca	pale-meat sausage.
morcillo	fleshy part of leg.
meat cut	*see diagrams from page 166 on.*
morcillón	scallops.
morcón	large black pudding.
morera	mulberry.
morraguete	mullet.
morrillo	nape of neck (cattle).
meat cut	*see diagrams from page 166 on.*
morrón	sweet pepper.
mortadela	pork sausage.
mortero	mortar.
mostaza	mustard.
mosto	must (fermenting grape juice).
mover	to stir gently.
moya	fish of the cod family.
muergo	sword razor (shellfish).
mueve ligeramente	stir gently.
múgil	mullet.
mújol	mullet.

muslo	drumstick; thigh.
muy	very.
hecho	well done.

Naba	swede.
nabo\nabon (de mesa)	turnip.
ñame	yam.
naranjas	oranges.
de\para postre	sweet oranges.
gajo	segment.
sanguina	blood oranges.
nariz	bouquet of wine (nose).
nata	cream.
enriquecida	double cream.
liquida	single cream.
montada	whipped cream.
para cocinar	for cooking.
para montar	for whipping.
natarón	cottage cheese.
natillas	custard.
de huevo	egg custard.
navaja	razor shellfish.
nécora	crab.
nectar de (fruit)	sweetened fruit juices.
nectarina	nectarine.
negro	black.
nevera	refrigerator.
nidos	noodles.
nískalos	wild mushrooms.
no ahumado	unsmoked.
no congelar de nuevo	do not refreeze.
no es necesario descongelar	cook from frozen.
no lechero	non-dairy.
ñoquis	dumplings.
ñoras	sweet chile peppers.
noviembre	November.

no volver a congelar
	una vez descongelado ...... do not refreeze once defrosted.
nueces .... nuts; walnuts.
	de California .... walnuts.
nuevo de ebullicíon .... bring back to the boil.
nuez .... nut; walnut.
	de mantequilla .... knob of butter.
	de marañon .... brazil nut.
	moscada .... nutmeg.

Objetos de cobre .... copperware.
oblea .... wafer.
oca .... goose.
octubre .... October.
odre .... wineskin.
ojal .... grommet; pressure valve.
oleoso .... oily.
oliva .... olive.
olla .... stewpot.
	presión .... pressure cooker.
omelet .... omelette.
oporto .... port.
orden .... order; sequence.
ordeñar .... to milk.
orégano .... oregano.
orejas .... ears.
orejones .... dried apricots\peaches;
	dried cored apple rings.
orgánico .... organic.
orozuz .... liquorice.
ortega .... grouse.
orujo .... peel of pressed grapes or olives.
ossobuco .... veal shank slice.
ostión .... Portuguese oyster.
ostra .... common oyster.
	japonesa .... pacific oyster.
otoño .... Autumn.

oveja	sheep.
leche de oveja	sheep's milk.
queso de oveja	sheep's milk cheese.
ovoso	full of roe.

Pacana	pecan.
paella	rice dish.
pagel	bream.
paja para tomar	drinking straws.
paleadar	to savour.
paleta	shoulder; fish slice.
de cordero	shoulder of lamb.
meat cut	*see diagrams from page 166 on.*
paletilla	shoulder.
meat cut	*see diagrams from page 166 on.*
palillos	cocktail sticks; toothpicks.
palito	skewer; skewered.
palitos de queso	cheese straws.
paloma	dove; pigeon.
torcaz	wood pigeon.
palometa roja	red bream.
palomitas (de maiz)	popcorn.
palote	rolling pin.
palta	avocado.
pámpana	vineleaf.
pan	bread.
ácimo	unleavened bread.
bazo	brown bread.
casero	homemade bread.
cornero de pan	crust; heel.
de boda	wedding cake.
de centeno	rye bread.
de higos	fig tart.
de molde	bread baked in a mould.
de pasas	fruitloaf.
duro	stale bread.
inglés	"tin".
integral	brown\wholemeal bread.

migas de pan	croûtons; breadcrumbs.
rebanado	sliced bread.
rallado	breadcrumbs.
sin cortar	uncut.
sin corteza	without crust.
tierno	fresh bread.
tostado	toast.
panadería	bakery.
panadero	baker.
panal	honeycomb.
panceta	bacon.
(not cured)	belly pork.
meat cut	*see diagrams from page 166 on.*
pancito	sugar lump.
panecillo	muffin; bread roll.
panera	bread basket.
panizo	maize.
panoja	corncob.
panqueque	pancake.
papas	potatoes.
fritas	french fries.
papaya	pawpaw.
papel	paper.
aluminio	aluminium foil.
de cocina	kitchen paper.
de estaño	tinfoil.
vegetal	greaseproof paper.
papilla	porridge.
papita	chip.
para	for; in order to.
decorar	for decoration\garnish.
evitar	in order to get.
llevar	takeaway.
montar	for whipping (cream).
que espese	for thickening.
parcialmente	partially.
pareja	brace (of game).
pargo	large red\sea bream.

parilla	grill; griddle.
parra	vine.
parrillada	grilled; mixed grill.
parro	duck.
partes iguales	equal parts.
partir	divide; cleave; cut.
pasa	dried fruit.
pasado	old; stale; off.
pasapure	food mill.
pasar por la licuadora	blend.
pasarlos	pass them (through).
pasas	currants; raisins.
de Corinto	currants.
de Esmirna	sultanas\yellow raisins.
uvas	raisins.
pase por harina	roll in flour.
pasta	paste; dough; noodle.
alimenticia	pasta.
(para) rebozar	batter.
pastas	biscuits.
pastel	cake; fruit pie\pasty.
de queso	cheesecake.
pasterizada	pasteurised.
pastilla de caldo	stock cube.
de pescado	fish stock cube.
de carne	meat stock cube.
de vegetal	vegetable stock cube.
pastilla encendido	firelighter.
pastinaca	parsnip.
pastoso	doughy.
pata	leg of animal.
patatas	potatoes.
asada	roast potatoes.
cocida	boiled potatoes.
en polvo	powdered mashed potato.
fecula de patata	potato starch.
fritas	chips; crisps.

pela de patatas	potato peeler.
puré de patatas	mashed potatoes.
paté	paté.
patitos	duckling.
pato	duck.
patudo	bigeye tuna.
pava	turkey hen.
pavipollo	large chicken.
pavo	turkey.
pebre	garlic\pepper sauce.
pecho	breast of mammal.
meat cut	*see diagrams from page 166 on.*
pechuga	breast of bird.
pectina	pectin.
pedacitos	small pieces; flakes.
en pedacitos	flaked.
pedacitos de carne	crackling; scratchings.
pegote	thick stew.
peje	fish (general).
sapo	angler fish.
pela de patatas	potato peeler.
peladillas	sugared almonds.
pelado	peeled; skinned.
pelador	peeler.
pelar	to peel.
pelarlos	peel them.
pele	peel.
pellejo	wineskin.
penca	prickly pear.
pepinillo	pickled dill; gherkin.
pepino	cucumber.
blanco	short cucumber.
Hollandes	long cucumber.
pepita	pip; seed.
pepitoria	stew.
pepitoso	full of pips.
pepón	water melon.
pequeño	small.

pera	pear.
perada	pear jam.
perca	perch.
percebes	goose barnacles.
percolador	percolator.
perdiz	partridge.
perejil	parsley.
perifollo	chervil.
perilla	small pear.
pernil	ham; gammon; leg.
pesar	to weigh.
pescada	hake.
pescadería	fish market.
pescadilla	whiting; young hake.
pescado	fish (all, dead).
menudo	whitebait.
pescador	fishmonger.
pescaito	mixed fried fish.
pescuezo	neck.
meat cut	*see diagrams from page 166 on.*
peso	weight.
bruto	gross weight.
neto	net weight.
pestiños	fried fish.
pez	fish (all, alive).
angel	angelfish.
de limón	silver fish.
espada	swordfish.
martillo	hammerhead shark.
picada	mince.
picadillo	mince.
picadillo de	minced; ground.
picado	minced; chopped; ground.
picante	hot (highly seasoned).
picantón	pullet.
picar	to chop; mince.
picarlos	mince them.
picatostes	croûtons.

pichon	pigeon.
piel	skin; peel.
crujiente de cerdo	crackling.
pierna	leg.
pies de cerdo	pigs' trotters.
pieza	piece; portion.
pijota	hake.
pilongas	dried chestnuts.
pimentero	pepper shaker.
pimentón (húngaro)	paprika.
pimienta	pepper; peppercorns.
colorado	paprika.
de cayenna	cayenne pepper.
de Jamaica	allspice.
inglesa	allspice.
rosa	red peppercorns.
pimiento	peppers; capsicum.
de cometilla	hot peppers.
morrones	red pepper; sweet pepper.
rojo	red pepper.
verde	green pepper.
pimpollo	sprig.
piña	pineapple.
en rodajas	pineapple rings.
en trozos	pineapple chunks.
pincel de cocina	pastry brush.
pinchar	to prick\puncture.
pinchitos	snacks; savoury tidbits.
pinchos	snacks.
morunos	kebabs.
piñonate	candied pine nut.
piñones	pine nuts.
pintada	guinea fowl.
pinzas	tongs.
pipas	pips; seeds.
pipote	keg.
pistacho	pistachio.
pistadero	pestle.

pistar	to pound with a pestle.
pistiñes	biscuits.
pisto	ratatouille.
pitorra	woodcock.
pizca	a pinch of.
plancha	grill plate.
plástico para envolver	clingfilm; Saran wrap.
plastón de	dollop of.
plata labrada	silverware.
plátanos	bananas.
platija	flounder; plaice; sole.
platillo	plate; saucer.
plato	plate; course; dish.
fuente	large plate.
hondo	deep plate.
llano	small dinner plate.
postre	side plate.
primer (1°) plato	first course.
segundo (2°) plato	second\main course.
platos	dishes; meals.
plegado	folding; plaiting.
pochar	to fry until soft.
pochas	beans; kidney beans.
pocho	overripe.
pochos	haricot beans.
poco	little; few.
hecho	rare; underdone.
polenta	maize gruel.
poleo	mint; pennyroyal.
pollastra	pullet.
pollita	young chicken.
pollo	chicken.
alas de pollo	chicken wings.
asado	roast (usually on a spit).
campero	free range chicken.
de corral	farmyard chicken.
muslos de pollo	chicken drumsticks.

pechuga de pollo	breast of chicken.
trocitos de pollo	chicken nuggets.
polvo	powder.
en polvo	powdered\ground.
polvorones	small cakes\biscuits.
pomelo	grapefruit.
ponchada	bowl of punch.
ponche	punch.
pondremos al fuego	put on to heat.
poner	to put\add\arrange.
la mesa	set the table.
ponga	put; add.
ponga a remojar	put in to soak.
pongalos a macerar	put them to soak.
por cabeza	per head.
porcino	piglet.
porción	portion; share; part.
por la mitad	through the centre.
poroto	bean.
porreta	green leaf of onion\leek.
porrino	baby leek.
porro	leek.
porron	jug; wine jar.
portavasos	coaster.
posada	cutlery case.
posar	to settle (of liquids).
poscafé	liqueur coffee.
poso	sediment.
posta	slice of meat.
postre	dessert.
cuchara de postre	dessert spoon.
naranjas para postre	sweet oranges.
pota	squid.
potable	drinkable.
potaje	vegetable soup\stew.
potajeria	vegetable shop.
pote	pot; jug; jar.
galledo	vegetable broth.

potenciador del sabor	flavour enhancer (MSG).
potestativo	optional.
pozol\pozole	vegetable stew.
precalentar	preheat.
precio del cubierto	cover charge.
precocinado	precooked.
preferencias	preferences.
prensa ajos	garlic press.
prensar	to press\squeeze.
preparado	prepared; pre-cooked.
preparar	to prepare\get ready.
prevenido	ready.
previamente ajuagado	previously rinsed.
primavera	Spring.
primer plato	first course.
pringar	dip in grease.
pringoso	greasy.
pringue	grease; dripping.
pringuera	rendering pan.
prisco	peach.
probar	to taste a little of.
propano	propane.
propina	tip (gratuity).
propinar	to invite for a drink.
proteínas	proteins.
de leche	milk proteins.
proveer	to supply\stock.
provisión de alimento	catering.
pruna	prune.
puchera	cooking pot.
puchero	stew; casserole; stewed.
puches	porridge.
pudín	pudding.
puedan ir al horno	oven-proof.
puerco	pig; pork.
montés	wild boar.
puerro	leek.
pulpa	pulp; flesh.

pulpeta	slice of meat.
pulpitos	baby octopus.
pulpo	common octopus.
amizclado	musky octopus.
blanco	curled octopus.
patudo	long legged octopus.
puñado	handful.
punchar	to prick.
punta de ebullición	boiling point.
puntas de bambú	bamboo shoots.
puntas de espárragos	asparagus tips.
puntillitas	baby squids.
puré	purée.
de patatas	mashed potato.
purpurea	burdock.
purrela	plonk.
Quemada	caramelised.
quemador	burner ring on cooker.
quesadilla	cheesecake.
quesera	cheesedish.
queso	cheese.
añejo	matured.
azul	blue cheese.
bandeja de queso	cheeseboard.
blando	soft cheese.
curada	cured.
de bola	round cheese (as edam).
de cabra	goat's milk cheese.
de oveja	sheep's milk cheese.
de vaca	cow's milk cheese.
especial para	specially for.
fundido	melted cheese.
palitos de queso	cheese straws.
parmesano	parmesan.
pastel de queso	cheesecake.
rallado	grated cheese.

continued / seguido

queso (*continued / seguido*)
- semicurada ...... semicured.
- suave ...... mild.
- tierno ...... young.
- viejo ...... matured (old).

quinto ...... small bottle of beer.
quisquilla ...... shrimp.
quitar ...... to remove.
quite ...... remove.

Rabada ...... rump.
rabanito ...... radish.
rábano ...... radish.
- picante ...... horseradish.

rabazuz ...... liquorice juice.
rabillo (*meat cut*) ...... *see diagrams from page 166 on.*
rabo ...... tail.
- de buey ...... ox tail.

ración ...... serving; portion.
racionador helado ...... ice-cream scoop.
raciones ...... servings.
raigal ...... root.
raja ...... slice (of fruit).
rajar ...... to split.
rallado ...... grated.
rallador ...... grater.
rallar ...... to grate.
ramillettes de hierbas
- aromaticas ...... bouquet garni.

ramita ...... sprig; floret.
ramo ...... string (of onions, etc)
rana común ...... edible frog.
- ancas de rana ...... frog's legs.

ranche ...... plain food; farm.
rangifero ...... reindeer.
rape ...... monkfish; angler fish.
rápida ...... fast-acting.
raquis ...... spine.

rasa/raso	level (spoonful).
rasar	to skim.
rascascio	rock cod.
raspador limón	lemon zester.
rastra	string of garlic\onions, etc.
raya	skate.
alas de raya	skate wings.
rebanada	a slice.
rebanaditas tostada	croûtons.
rebanado	sliced.
rebanador	slicing machine.
rebanar	to slice.
rebozadas	fried in batter.
rebozado	battered.
rebozar	to coat with batter, etc.
recalentar	to heat\warm up.
recambio	refill.
recentar	to add yeast.
receta	recipe.
recetario	recipe book.
recipiente	container.
recocer	reheat; reboil; overcook.
recocina	pantry.
reconstituida	reconstituted.
recortar	to cut off\trim.
rectificar	to rectify\make right.
de sal	season to taste.
redondo	round (meat cut)
de carne	joint of meat.
reducción	reduction.
reducir	to reduce\decrease.
reenvasar	to refill.
refección	snack.
refinado	refined.
refreir	re-fry.
refrescante	refreshing.
refrescar	to refresh\cool.

refrescarlos	refresh them.
refrescos	soft drinks.
refrigerador	refrigerator.
refrigerar	to cool.
refrito	hash; overfried.
regaifa	Easter cake.
regaliz	liquorice.
regimén (dietica) especiál	diet.
regoldana	horse chestnut.
rehogar	to braise\brown.
rejilla	cooling rack; grille.
rellenado\rellenas	stuffed.
rellenar	to fill; stuff.
relleno	stuffing; filling.
reloj de arena	egg timer.
remojar	soak; steep.
remolacha	beetroot.
azucarera	sugar beet.
cocida	cooked beetroot.
remover	to stir.
remover varias veces	stir occasionally.
removiendo	stirring.
al mismo tiempo	stirring at the same time.
bien	stirring well.
continuamente	stirring continuously.
remueva	stir.
de vez en cuando	stirring occasionally.
reo	sea trout.
repartir	distribute; apportion.
repicar	to mince\chop.
repleto	full-up\sated.
repollo	cabbage.
liso	drumhead cabbage.
rizado	savoy cabbage.
reposar	to rest.
reposte	larder.
repostería	confectionery; pastry shop.
reposteria	buffet.

requemar	to overcook\taste hot.
requesón	cream cheese.
granulado	cottage cheese.
res	head of cattle.
reserva	aged (wine).
reservar	put to one side.
reservarla en la nevera	store in the fridge.
resfriada	fridge.
resfriar	to chill.
resquemo	taste\smell of burnt food.
restante	the rest of; remaining.
restaurante	restaurant.
resto	leftovers.
retir\ario\er del fuego	remove from the heat.
retirar	remove; put aside.
revolver	turn over; stir.
revueltos	scrambled egg dishes.
rico	rich; delicious; tasty.
en	rich in.
riñonada	kidney dish; a chop with kidney.
meat cut	*see diagrams from page 166 on.*
riñones	kidneys.
rioja	wine-growing region.
ristra	string of garlic\onions.
rizado	curly.
róbalo	haddock; sea bass; turbot.
rociar	sprinkle; spray; douse.
rocíelas con	spray them with.
rodaballo	turbot.
rodajas	round slices.
finas	thinly sliced rings.
rodillo	rolling pin.
rojo	red.
rollo	rolling pin.
romero	rosemary.
ron	rum.
roncha	slice.
rosada	red snapper.

rosbif	roast beef.
roscon	ring-shaped cake.
roscos	sweet rings; doughnuts.
rosetas	popcorn.
rosquilla	coffee cake; doughnut; ring-shaped cake.
rosquillos	spirals.
rovellón	wild mushroom.
rubio	red gurnard.
rucola	rocket\arugula.
rueda	round slice.
ruibarbo	rhubarb.
russo	Russian.
Sabor	flavour; taste.
saborear	to flavour\relish\enjoy.
sabroso	tasty; savoury; delicious.
sacacorchos	corkscrew.
sacar	to extract\remove.
sacarina	saccharine.
sacudir	shake.
sagu	sago.
sajar	to slice open.
sal	salt.
marina\del mar	sea salt.
salado	savoury; salted; salty.
saladura	salting; curing with salt.
salar	to salt\season.
salazón	salted; cured.
salchicha	sausage (veal\pork).
salchichon	large sausage (pork); salami.
salcochar	to boil in salted water.
salero	salt cellar\shaker.
salmón	salmon.
salmonete	red mullet.
salmuera	brine.
salón de té	tearoom.
salpicar	sprinkle.

salpicón	chopped meat with onions etc.
de mariscos	seafood cocktail.
salpimentar	to season (salt & pepper).
salsa	sauce; dressing; gravy.
agridulce	sweet & sour sauce.
bechamel	bechamel sauce.
de barbacoa	barbecue sauce.
rosa	thousand island dressing.
de tomate	tomato sauce.
salsera	gravy boat; saucer.
salteado	sautéed.
saltear	to sauté.
salud	health.
saludable	healthy; wholesome.
salva	tray; salver.
salvado	bran.
salvamantel	place mat.
salvático	wild.
salvia	sage.
salvilla	salver; tray.
sancochar	parboil.
sandía	water melon.
sangre	blood.
sangria	drink with base of red wine and orange juice.
sanguesa	raspberry.
San Pedro	John Dory.
sanwich	sandwich.
sanwichera	sandwich maker; toaster.
sardinas	sardines.
sardineta	small sardine.
sardinillas	small sardines.
sarilla	marjoram.
sarria	fruit basket.
sartén	frying pan.
sarteneja	small frying pan.
sativo	cultivated.
sazon	ripeness.

sazonador	seasoning.
sazonar	to season\ripen.
sebo	suet.
sec\seca\seco	dry.
secar	to dry.
secarlos	dry them.
se compone	consists of.
sed	thirst; dryness.
seguidamente	subsequently; following.
según	according to.
peso	by weight.
segundo plato	second\main course.
seleccion	selection; choice.
sellar	to seal\close.
sélvatico	wild.
semicubrir	partially cover.
semidesnatada	semi-skimmed.
semidulce	medium sweet.
semilla	seed.
semi-seco	semi-dry.
sémol\sémola	semolina.
sepia	cuttlefish.
septiembre	September.
sequete	stale bread.
sequillo	rusk.
serrano ham	raw cured ham.
servicio	set of (servicio de té = teaset)
servilleta	napkin.
servilletero	napkin ring.
servir	to serve.
bien caliente	serve hot.
en seguida	serve at once.
sesada	fried brains.
sésamo	sesame.
sesos	brains.
setas	wild mushrooms.
sharon	persimmon.
sidra	cider.

sifón	....	syphon; soda syphon.
siluro	....	catfish.
silvestre	....	uncultivated; wild.
sin	....	without.
burbujas	....	still (drink).
dejar de batir	....	beating continuously.
dejar de remover	....	stirring continuously.
gas	....	still (drink).
huesos	....	without bones\seeds, etc.
nada de grasa	....	without additional fat\oil.
pepitas	....	without pips.
sínfito	....	comfrey.
sirope	....	syrup.
sitio	....	a place.
templado	....	a warm place.
soasar	....	to roast lightly.
sobadora	....	kneading\rubbing.
sobre	....	packet; sachet.
sobreasar	....	to roast again.
sobrecomida	....	dessert.
sobremesa	....	tablecloth; dessert.
(de sobremesa)	....	post-prandial.
sobresada	....	sausage (pork).
soda	....	soda.
sofreir	....	fry gently.
sofreirlos	....	fry them gently.
soja	....	soya.
blanca	....	soya bean.
germinada	....	beansprouts.
verde	....	mung beans.
solidos lacteos	....	milk solids.
solla\solleta	....	flounder; plaice.
sollo	....	sturgeon.
solomillo	....	fillet steak; sirloin; rump.
de cerdo	....	pork fillet.
sonrosado	....	pink.
sopa	....	soup.
de rabo de buey	....	ox tail soup.

sopera	soup tureen.
sopero	soup plate.
sopita	light soup.
sosa	soda.
suave	smooth; mild.
subir	to rise.
suera	whey.
de leche	buttermilk; whey.
en polvo	whey powder.
suflé	soufflé.
suizo	bun.
sumergir	immerse.
supermercado	supermarket.
suplemento	extra helping; seconds.
surtido	assorted; assortment.
suspiros	meringues.

Tabla cortar	chopping board.
taco	plug; bung; stopper.
tailandés	Thai.
tajada	steak; a slice.
tajadera	large knife.
tajadero	chopping block.
tajar	to slice.
tajon	chopping block.
tallarines	noodles.
tallos	stalk; stem.
de cebolleta	chives.
tamal	meat pasty.
tamaño	size.
tamarindo	tamarind.
tamiz	sieve; flour dredger.
tamizado	strained; liquidised and strained.
tamizar	to sieve\sift.
tapa	lid; small serving.
meat cut	*see diagrams from page 166 on.*
tapana	caper.

tapar		to cover.
	la cacuela	cover the pan.
	parcialmente	partially cover.
tapas		small serving.
tápelo		cover.
tapete		tablecloth.
tapon cava		champagne stopper.
tapones de palanca		bottle stoppers with lever.
tarascon		a mouthful\bite.
tarro		jar; bottle.
tarta		tart; sweet pie.
	de manzana	apple pie.
tartaletta		tart.
tártaro		tartar; cream of tartar.
tartera		baking tray.
tarugo		wooden bung.
tasajo		slice of meat; hung beef; jerked beef.
taza		cup; bowl; basin.
	de té	teacup; cup of tea.
tazon		bowl.
	bol mezclas	mixing bowl.
té		tea.
	bolsita de té	teabag.
	chino	China tea.
	salon de té	tearoom.
	taza de té	cup of tea.
	verde	green tea.
teina		caffeine.
telina		clam.
témpano		side of bacon\cured pork.
templado		warm; tepid.
tenacillas		tongs.
tenaza		pincer (lobster\crab); claw.
tenca		tench.
tendero		shopkeeper.
tenedor		fork.
termos		thermos flask.
ternasco		roast young lamb.

ternera	veal (*but see* Introduction).
añojo	yearling.
blanca	young.
de Avila	young.
joven	young.
lechal	young.
menor	young.
terrón de azúcar	sugar lump.
tetera	teapot.
tetero	feeding bottle.
tetilla	teat of feeding bottle.
tibio	tepid; lukewarm.
tiburón	shark.
tiempo	time; room temperature.
de cocción	cooking time.
de horneado	baking time.
tienda	shop.
de comestibles	grocery store.
de alimentos dietéticos	health food store.
tiene visios de	it has the appearance of.
tierno	tender; soft; fresh (bread).
tijeras	scissors.
tila	linden flower.
tintilla	sweet red wine.
tintillo	pale wine.
tirabeques	mange tout.
tirabuzon	corkscrew.
tiras	strips.
tisana	infusion.
toballeta	napkin.
tocino	pork fat; lard; salt pork; fatty; bacon (back).
de cielo	sweet of syrup and eggs.
tomar	to take\have.
tomate	tomato.
concentrado	tomato paste.
frito	puréed tomato.
pelado entero	whole peeled tomato.

pera	plum tomato.
salsa de tomate	tomato ketchup; catsup.
tamizado	puréed and sieved.
triturado	reduced puréed tomato.
troceado	chopped tomatoes.
tomillo	thyme.
toña	large loaf.
tonel	barrel; cask.
tonelete	keg.
tonica	tonic.
toro	uncastrated bull.
de lídia	bull killed in ring.
toronja	grapefruit.
torrar	to toast.
torrezno	slice of bacon.
torrijas	baked, sweet bread slices.
torta	tart; pie.
de avena	oatcake.
tortada	meat pie.
tortel	bun.
tortera	pie dish; baking dish.
tortilla	omelette (*but see* Introduction).
francesa	egg-only omelette.
tortillitas	fritters; fish fritters.
tortita	waffle; pancake.
tortuga	turtle.
tostada	toast.
tostado	toasted.
tostar	to toast.
tostón	roast suckling pig.
tournedo	steak.
trabajar	work; rub (pastry).
transvasar	to decant.
trapiche	olive press.
trascolar	to strain\filter.
traseros	rump; rear section.
trasmosto	plonk.
traste	glass for wine tasting.

tras unos minutos	after a few minutes.
trébedes	trivet.
trigo	wheat.
germen de trigo	wheatgerm.
harina de trigo	wheat flour.
inflado	puffed wheat.
trinchar	to carve.
trinche	fork.
trinchete	fruit knife.
tripa	sausage skin.
tritura	liquidise; mash.
triturado	liquidised.
triturar	to mash\crunch\liquidise.
triturarlos	pulverise\liquidise them.
trocear	to cut into cubes\pieces.
trocito	small cube; knob (butter).
de pollo	chicken nugget.
trofito de mantequilla	knob of butter.
tronquitos del mar	crabsticks.
trozo	piece; chunk; nugget.
trucha	trout.
arco iris	rainbow trout.
del mar	sea trout.
trufados	truffles (sweet).
trufar	to stuff with truffles.
trufas	truffles (funghi).
trujal	oil press.
tuétano	marrow (of bone).
tumbet	a casserole.
tupinambo	Jerusalem artichoke.
turma	testicle.
de tierra	truffle.
turrar	to roast.
turrón	nougat *(but see* Introduction).

Ubre	udder.
ucar	pound; grind.
ultracongelar	deep frozen.

un par de	equal amount of.
una vez finalizada	when finished.
una vez pelado	once peeled.
unos	some; a few.
minutos	a few minutes.
untar	to spread\grease.
unte el fondo	grease the base.
unto	lard; fat.
urogallo	grouse.
uva espina	gooseberry.
uvas	grapes.
de Corinto	currants.
pasas	sultanas; raisins.

Vaca	cow.
vaciador fruta	melon baller.
vaciar	to empty.
vacíe	drain.
vacio	empty.
vacuna	beef.
menor	young beef (veal).
vaina	pod.
vainilla	vanilla.
vajilla de plata	silverware.
vajillas	dishes; pots & pans.
vapor	steam.
varillas	wire\balloon whisk.
varitas de (fish)	fish fingers.
vasija	jar.
vaso	glass; tumbler.
para vino	wineglass.
vegetal	vegetable.
vegetalista	vegetarian.
vegetariano	vegetarian.
vélada	dinner party.
venado (carne de)	venison; deer.
vendimia	vintage; grape harvest.
verano	Summer.

verde	green.
verdel	mackerel.
verdulero	greengrocer.
verduras	vegetables; greens.
ver envase	see package.
vermut	vermouth.
verter	to pour\empty.
encima	pour over the top.
viandas	food.
vid	vine.
vieira	scallop.
viejo	old.
vierta	pour; empty; sprinkle.
vierte el contenido	empty the contents.
viñador	wine grower.
vinagre	vinegar.
vinagrera	vinegar bottle.
vinagreta	vinegar-based sauce.
vinazo	strong wine.
vincapervinca	periwinkle.
vinillo	weak wine.
vino	wine.
blanco	white wine.
carta de vinos	winelist.
copa\vaso de vino	wineglass; glass of wine.
cubo para vino	wine bucket.
de la casa	house wine.
de solera	vintage wine.
de verez	sherry.
dulce	sweet wine.
rosado	rosé wine.
seco	dry wine.
tinto	red wine.
víveres	food; provisions.
volador	squid.
volandeira	queen scallop.
volatería	poultry.
volcar	overturn; tip out; upend.

volovan	vol au vent.
voltear	to turn over.
volumen	part (quantity ratios).
volver	turn up\over\down.
vuelve	return it.

Whiski .... whisky; scotch.
    americano .... bourbon.

Ya .... now; already.
yema .... egg yolk; bud.
yemas .... fondants.
    de espárragos .... asparagus tips.
yerba .... herb.
yerbabuena .... mint.
yogur .... yoghurt.
yogurtera .... yoghurt maker.

Zamburiña .... scallop.
zanahoria .... carrot.
zancarrón .... large leg bone.
zapallo .... pumpkin; gourd.
zaque .... wineskin.
zarza .... blackberry.
zarzamora .... blackberry.
zarzaparilla .... sarsaparilla.
zumo .... juice.
zumoso .... juicy.
zurrapa .... dregs.

__Wine__

abocado	medium dry; smooth.
afrutado	fruity.
apellido	named.
autóctona	native to.
barrica	cask.
blanco	white.
bodega	wine cellar.
de origen	cellar of grape grower.
catavinos	wine-taster.
cava	sparkling wine.
clarete	claret.
cosecha	crop.
crianza	aged in wooden barrels.
CVC	mixed vintage; blended.
(*conjunto de varias cosechas*)	
de la tierra	local to areas named.
DO	quality controlled.
(*denominacion de origen*)	
DOC	quality controlled.
(*denominacion de origen clasificada*)	
eleborado	produced; made.
embotellado	bottled.
envejecido	aged.
gastronomía	food serve-with advice.
generoso	full bodied.
nariz	bouquet.
pellejo	wine skin.
poso	sediment.
roble	oak.
rosada	rosé.
sin crianza	unclassified.
tinto	red.

uva	grape.
vaso para vino	wineglass.
viña	vineyard.
viñador	wine grower.
vinatero	wine merchant.
vinaza	inferior wine.
vinazo	strong wine.
viñedo	vineyard.
vinicultura	wine growing.
vinillo	thin\weak wine.
vino	wine.
de pasto	table wine.
generoso	fine\dessert wine.
zona	region.

Wine Sweetness Scale

DRY → SWEET

brut   seco   semiseco   semidulce   dulce

Cava (sparkling wine) also uses the term ***brut de brut***, which means drier than *brut*.

Shopping

The following list of words and phrases will give you confidence when buying and getting information from shop staff.

By mixing and matching you may not produce grammatically correct sentences, but you will be understood if you keep it simple. Pidgin is fine - communication is the goal.

Try to ask questions which will bring a response that you will understand, preferably yes or no. For example, don't ask *when* something will be in stock because you probably won't understand the answer, ask if it will be, "Here tomorrow/the day after tomorrow/Monday?" (***"Aqui mañana/pasado manana/Lunes?"***)

In Spanish, the difference between a question, "Do you have frog's legs?" – *«¿Tiene ancas de rana?»*, and a statement, "You have frog's legs." – *«Tiene ancas de rana.»*, can be entirely in the inflection. When asking a question, make it ***sound*** like a question, and make a questioning face, otherwise he may just think you are insulting his perfectly normal legs.

Miming is fine, provided you can do it and it means something. Obscure, meaningless gestures will only add confusion. Play Charades the week before flying.

If anything is met with a truly blank response, think of another way of saying it. If the words were correct re-read the pronunciation guides – or show them the relevant part of the book.

It is always a good idea to prepare the important words beforehand. Write down key words and complicated questions, and include any alternative words.

Try to pre-empt answers and be ready with a response.

Shopping: English/Spanish.

a	un\una.
a couple of	un par de.
a few	unos.
afternoon	tarde.
ago: 2 hours ago	hace dos horas.
2 days ago	hace dos dias.
2 months ago	hace dos meses.
a little more	un poco más.
almost	por poco.
also	también.
another	otro.
as soon as possible	lo antes posible.
available	disponible.
bag	bolsa.
bank	banco.
bank holiday	día festivo.
before	antes.
best (the)	lo mejor.
better	mejor.
bigger	más grande.
bill	factura.
the bill	la cuenta.
both	ambos.
bought (I bought)	Yo compré.
broken	roto.
but	pero.
Can I ...?	Puedo ...?
Can I have …?	Puedo darme …?
Can I see?	Puedo ver?
Can you ...?	Puede usted ...?
Can you get ...?	Obtiene usted ...?
cash	efectivo.
change	cambio.
cheap	barato.
cheaper	más barato.

149

checkout	caja.
date (time)	fecha.
day	día.
after tomorrow	pasado mañana.
before yesterday	anteayer.
deliver	entregar.
different	diferente.
down	abajo.
Do you have ...?	Tiene...?
anything cheaper?	algo más barato?
Do you know ...?	Sabe...?
each	cada.
elevator	ascensor.
enough	bastante.
entrance	entrada.
evening	tarde.
exchange	cambio.
exit	salida.
expensive	caro.
few	pocos.
Fire Exit	Salida de Emergencia.
for	para.
Friday	viernes.
from (place)	de.
It is from here	Es de aquí.
from (sequence/since)	desde.
all from one euro	todo desde un euro.
open from 2 to 4	abierto desde 2 a 4.
good	bueno.
half	medio.
an hour	medio hora.
handful	puñado.
he	él.
help	ayuda.
Help me, please	Ayudame por favor.
her	ella.
here	aqui.

him	él.
home delivery	reparto a domicilio.
How much are these\those?	Cuánto cuestan estos\esos?
How much is it?	Cuánto es?
I bought	Yo compré.
I don't know	No sé.
I don't understand	No entiendo.
if	si.
I like	Me gusta.
I'll return tomorrow	Vuelvo mañana.
I'll wait	Espero.
I'm looking for	Buscando para.
important	importante.
I'm sorry	Lo siento.
I need	Necesito.
instead of	en vez de.
invoice	factura.
is it possible?	es posible?
I take	Tomo.
it doesn't work	no función.
it is	es.
it isn't	no es.
I want	Quiero.
I want to pay	Quiero pagar.
I would like	Me gustaría.
just in case	por si acaso.
kilo	kilo.
large	grande.
last: night	anoche.
Monday	El lunes pasado.
month	mes pasada.
week	semana pasada.
later	más tarde.
left (direction)	izquierda.
less	menos.
lift (elevator)	ascensor.
litre	litro.

little, a	un poco.
lost	perdido.
many	muchos.
maybe	quizá.
May I see?	Puedo ver?
medium-sized	de tamaño mediano.
Monday	lunes.
money	dinero.
month	mes.
more	más.
more or less	más o menos.
morning	mañana.
much	mucho.
name	nombre.
necessary	necesario.
next (in order)	siguente.
next in line	siguente en linea.
next (in future)	próxima.
next Monday	el lunes próximo.
no	no.
none	ninguno.
noon	mediodía.
no one	nadie.
nothing	nada.
now	ahora.
number	numero.
of course	por supuesto.
only	solo.
open	abierto.
opening times	horario.
or	o.
other	otro.
paid	pagado.
pardon	perdón.
pay, to	pagar.
perfect	perfecto.
please	por favor.

Post Office	Correos.
price	precio.
quality	calidad.
quarter	cuarto.
receipt	recibo.
restroom	servicios.
return, to (give back to)	devolver.
return, to (revisit)	volver.
right (direction and privilege)	derecho.
same, the	al mismo.
Saturday	sabado.
she	ella.
shop	tienda.
show me.	mostrarme.
similar	similar.
similar to	parecido a.
size	tamaño.
slowly	despacio.
small	pequeño.
smaller	más pequeño.
some	algunos.
something	algo.
something else	otra cosa.
soon	pronto.
sooner	más pronto.
stock	repuesto.
stronger	más fuerte.
suggestions	sugerencias.
suitable	apropiado.
Sunday	domingo.
take, to	tomar.
takeaway	para llevar.
telephone	telefono.
tell me	digame.
thank you	gracias.
that	ese\esa.
that's all	completo.

the	....	el\la\los\las.
then	....	entonces.
there	....	alli.
these	....	estos\estas.
this	....	este\esta.
those	....	esos\esas.
Thursday	....	jueves.
today	....	hoy.
toilets	....	servicios.
ladies	....	señoras.
men	....	caballeros; hombres.
tomorrow	....	mañana.
afternoon	....	mañana por la tarde.
evening	....	mañana por la noche.
morning	....	mañana por la mañana.
tonight	....	esta noche.
too (also)	....	tambien
too (much)	....	demasiado.
early	....	demasiado temprano.
late	....	demasiado tarde.
Tuesday	....	martes.
twice as much	....	dos veces más.
up	....	arriba.
very	....	muy.
weaker	....	menos fuerte.
Wednesday	....	miercoles.
week	....	semana.
weekend	....	fin de semana.
what time ...?	....	que hora ...?
when?	....	cuándo?
where?	....	dónde?
Where can I buy...?	....	Dónde puedo comprar ...?
Where can I find...?	....	Dónde puedo encontrar…?
which?	....	cuál?
Will you wrap it for me?	....	Podria envolvermelo?
with	....	con.
without	....	sin.

wrapping paper	papel de envolver.
write it down, please.	por favor, escríbalo.
year	año.
yes	sí.
yesterday	ayer.
you	usted (formal); tú (friend/child).
You're very kind	Eres muy amable.

Shopping: Spanish/English.

abajo	down.
abierto	open.
algo mas?	Do you want anything else?
arriba	up.
ascensor	lift\elevator.
autoservicio	self-service.
banco	bank.
barato	cheap.
caballeros	men.
cada	each.
caja	checkout.
calidad	quality.
cambio	change; exchange.
cerrado	closed.
comprar	to buy.
con	with.
Correos	Post Office.
descuento	discount.
desde	from.
devolver	to return\give back to.
día	day.
día festivo	bank holiday.
disponible	available.
domingo	Sunday.
efectivo	cash.

155

empujar\empuje	push.
entrada	entrance.
espere su turno	wait your turn.
factura	invoice; bill.
fecha	date (time).
grande	large.
hombres	men.
horario	opening times.
jueves	Thursday.
kilo	kilogramme.
libro de reclamaciones	complaints book.
lunes	Monday.
martes	Tuesday.
más barato	cheaper.
miércoles	Wednesday.
numero	number.
offerta	offer.
pagado	paid.
pagar	to pay.
para llevar	takeaway.
piso	floor.
planta	floor.
por favor	please.
precio	price.
de costo	cost price.
de rebajado	sale price.
de venta al publico (PVP)	the retail price inc. tax.
próxima	next.
rebajas	sales; special offers.
recibo	receipt.
reparto a domicilio	home delivery.
repuesto	stock.
sábado	Saturday.
salida	exit.
Salida de Emergencia	Fire Exit.
semana	week.
señoras	ladies.

servicios	toilets\restroom.
sin	without.
solo	only.
sugerencias	suggestions.
tamaño	size.
ahorro	economy size.
telefono	telephone.
tirar	pull.
vender	to sell.
viernes	Friday.

Los Numeros

Numbers

Apart from 11 to 15, numbers are increased by simply linking additions. Say the whole as one word. If in doubt give the digits:

for example, say "uno cero tres" for 103.

Use of comma and decimal point is reversed in Spain; so 1,000 = 1.000 and 1.45 = 1,45

12.50 euros is often spoken as "doce con cincuenta"

zero	0	cero
one	1	uno
two	2	dos
three	3	tres
four	4	quatro
five	5	cinco
six	6	seis
seven	7	siete
eight	8	ocho
nine	9	nueve
ten	10	diez
eleven	11	once
twelve	12	doce
thirteen	13	trece
fourteen	14	catorce
fifteen	15	quince
sixteen	16	dieciseis
seventeen	17	diecisiete
eighteen	18	dieciocho
nineteen	19	diecinueve
twenty	20	veinte
twenty one	21	veintiuno
twenty two	22	veintidos

twenty three	23	veintitres
twenty four	24	veinticuatro
twenty five	25	veinticinco
	etc.	
thirty	30	treinte
forty	40	cuarenta
fifty	50	cincuenta
sixty	60	sesenta
seventy	70	setenta
eighty	80	ochenta
ninety	90	noventa
one hundred	100	cien
two hundred	200	doscientos
three hundred	300	trescientos
four hundred	400	cuatrocientos
five hundred	500	quinientos
six hundred	600	seiscientos
seven hundred	700	setecientos
eight hundred	800	ochocientos
nine hundred	900	novecientos
one thousand	1000	mil
two thousand	2000	dos mil
	etc.	
one million	1000000	un millon
two million	2000000	dos millones
	etc.	

First\1st .... 1ª \ 1°, primera\primero.
second\2nd .... 2ª \ 2°, segunda\o.
third\3rd .... 3°, tercero.
fourth\4th .... 4°, cuarto.
fifth\5th .... 5°, quinto.
sixth\6th .... 6°, sexto.
seventh\7th .... 7°, séptimo.
eighth\8th .... 8°, octavo.
ninth\9th .... 9°, noveno.
tenth\10th .... 10°, décimo.

Special Diets

A great deal of research has gone into the compilation of this book in general, and particularly into this section. However, it must be understood that it is not an authoritative medical text. Words and phrases included are those discovered or felt to be of value to those readers with special dietary needs, and appear only as a cautionary guide. Readers are recommended to seek professional medical advice where any doubt exists.

As you are likely to be away from home, and away from professional contacts when reading this, the website addresses given below should help you to arrive at a fast decision concerning the safety or otherwise of any included foodstuffs, as even small villages may have an internet café or shop.

Cooking is often described as an art. Chefs and cooks enjoy displaying their talents, but can be very secretive about ingredients, so gentle enquiries may not always provide the full details. You will need to explain why it is important that you know. If you do not explain exactly why it is important it may be assumed that you are simply being awkward, and staff may not become fully involved.

Remember also, though, that most people dislike showing ignorance, and that behind the apparently knowledgeable response may be a desire to hide that ignorance.

In reality, any food which does not arrive in any form of package which fully lists its ingredients cannot be deemed to be safe for anyone with any special dietary needs – particularly serious allergy responses.

Fill in the form on Page 170 with the Spanish translations of your particular unwelcome ingredients, and show it to anyone useful when needed.

<u>Allergies and Intolerances</u>

Labelling of potentially dangerous ingredients for those with allergies, and those with complaints such as coeliac disease, is happening, but is not yet common practice.

BE AWARE that where warnings are given, **"frutas secas" and "frutos secos" both mean nuts!** Frutas\os here is a general term, and does not refer solely to dried fruit.

Those who suffer with allergies will know that many sauces are created using wheat flour, but it is also common in Spain to use bread to thicken any type of sauce, stew, or soup. Ground nuts may also be used as a thickener, and whole or chopped nuts are commonly added to sauces, stews, and sausages to add flavour and texture.

Fortunately, many chemical terms are reasonably close to the English and are mostly readily recognisable, as, of course, are the E numbers.

Bajo en… means *Low in*…

Free, as in salt-free, sugar-free, etc, is in Spain simply *sin* (without), so "sin sal" and "sin azúcar".

Watch out, though, for such as:

SIN AZÚCAR, SIN SAL
añadido

The tiny *añadido* means *added*.

You may also see:

a   ñ   a   d   i   d   o

spread above, beneath, or through the larger, or emboldened *sin azucar, sin sal*, etc.

These misleading practices pass scrutiny because of Spanish grammar. Whereas in English the phrase would be, **without added sugar**, in Spanish the sequence is, **without sugar added** (***sin azúcar añadido***). The ***añadido*** correctly falls at the end, and some manufacturers appear to have taken full advantage of this. Where any such advice is displayed, look carefully for any accompanying ***añadido***.

Because such practices still exist, you must examine all texts carefully.

The following two helpful phrases, or similar, can be found on some packages.

Elaborada in una fábrica que utilizar: huevo, soja.
Produced in a factory that uses: egg, soya. (etc.)

Puede contener trazas de frutas secos (nueces).
May contain traces of nuts.

And occasionally, perhaps at the end of the ingredients lists, you may also find the advice:

Contiene gluten, trigo, huevo, soja.
Contains gluten, wheat, egg, soya. (etc.)

Relevant words and phrases

allergy	alergia.
allergic	alérgico.
because	porque.
dairy products	derivados lácteos.
dangerous	peligroso.
diabetes	diabetes.
diabetic	diabético.
diet, special	regimén especial.
Does it contain... ?	Contiene...?
Does it contain nuts?	Contiene nueces?
Do you have ...?	Tiene... ?
health	salud.
health problem	problema de salud.
high in	alto en.
I am allergic to ...	Soy alérgico a ...
I am diabetic.	Soy diabético.
I cannot eat...	No puedo comer ...
I have	Tengo.
I have a problem with...	Tengo problema con...
ill	enfermo.
I need to know ...	Necessito saber ...
insulin	insulina.
it is especially important	reviste especial importancia.
low in	bajo en.
What does it contain?	Que contiene?

Common problem foods and additives.

apple (peel)	manzana (piel de).
aspartame	aspartamo.
barley	cebada.
buckwheat	alforfón.
cheese	queso.

dairy	lechería.
products	derivados lácteos.
eggs	huevos.
flavour enhancer (MSG)	potenciador del sabor; monosidico glutamato.
flour	harina.
glucose syrup	jarabe de glucosa.
gluten	gluten.
grains	granos.
hydrogenated fat	grasa hidrogenada.
lactose	lactosa.
milk	leche.
cow's	leche de vaca.
goat's	leche de cabra.
sheep's	leche de oveja.
solids	solidos lacteos.
monosodium glutamate	monosidico glutamato; potenciador del sabor.
non-dairy	no lechero.
nuts	nueces; frutas secas.
on packets as	frutas secas (all).
almond	almendra.
brazil nut	castaña de brazil; coquito.
cashew nut	anacardo; marañon.
filbert	avellana.
groundnut	cacahuete; cuca; aráquida; maní.
hazelnut	avellana.
peanut	cacahuete; cuca; aráquida; maní.
pecan	pacana.
pine nuts	piñones.
tiger nut	chufa.
walnuts	nueces; nueces california.
oats	avena.
bread	pan.
peanut	cacahuete; cuca; aráquida; maní.
potato starch	fecula de patata.
rye	centeno.
shellfish	mariscos.

soy	soja.
starch	fecula; almidon.
sugar	azúcar.
sulphite	sulfito.
walnuts	nueces (de california).
wheat	trigo.
wheat starch	almidón de trigo.
whey powder	suera de leche en polvo.
yeast extract	extracto de levadura.

Lists of problem foods and other advice can be found at:

    www.food.gov.uk/healthiereating/allergyintol

    www.coeliac.co.uk

    www.fedupwithfoodadditives.info

Los Animales

MEAT CUTS

The following maps will help identify which part of the animal the Spanish cuts come from.

Some cuts from the same part of the animal differ in name. This is often simply because one is with bone, and the other without bone.

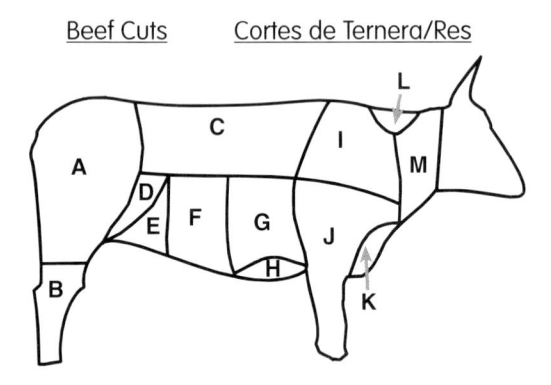

Beef Cuts   Cortes de Ternera/Res

A: cadera; tapilla; redondo; rabillo; tapa; contra tapa.
B: ossobucco; morcillos; culata de contra.
C: lomo; lomo bajo\alto; solomillo.
D: babilla.
E: rabillo de cadera.
F: falda.
G: costillar.
H: aleta.
I: aguja; lomo de aguja.
J: pez; espaldilla; brazuelo; morcillo; llana.
K: pecho.
L: morrillo.
M: pescuezo.

Pork Cuts   Cortes de Cerdo

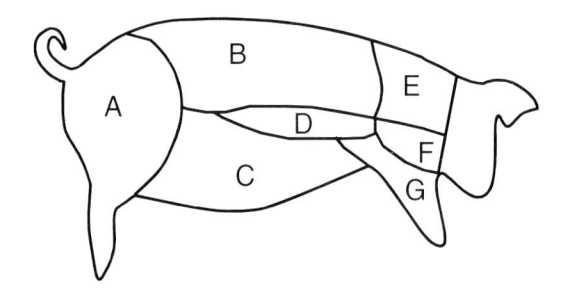

A: jamón.
B: lomo (cinta de); solomillo; tocino (lard).
C: costillar; panceta.
D: costillar; entraña.
E: cabezadas; aguja.
F: paleta; paletilla.
G: codillo.

Lamb Cuts   Cortes de Cordero

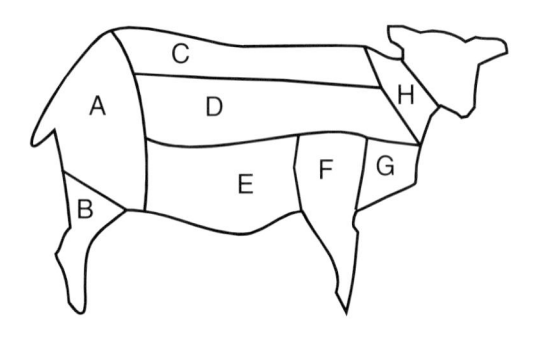

A: pierna.
B: pierna; codillo; garrón.
C: chuletas (de centro) de cordero.
D: costillar; costillas de cordero.
E: falda.
F: paletilla.
G: pecho.
H: pescuezo; cuello.

From the author.

Any input you feel inclined to give is always (hopefully) welcome, but omissions are particularly so. If something is missing that you feel should have been included, please let me know. This invitation extends to Spanish slang as well as nationally recognised terms, and also to U.S. English terms.

Please send your words, preferably with any extra information such as geographical location, frequency of use\hearing, etc., along with any suggestions or corrections to:

whitestreakpublishing@mail.com

Muchas gracias,

Paul.

Forthcoming Titles

Editions of the book are currently being compiled to include all the major ex-pat community languages existing in Spain - with Spanish as the common language.

Ayudame, por favor,

Necesito saber si estos platos contienen:

....

....

....

....

....

....

porque tengo alergia. Es muy importante para mi salud no comerlos.

Gracias.

This asks if any meals contain your problem foods, and explains why it is important that you know.

NOTES / NOTAS

NOTES / NOTAS

NOTES / NOTAS